BLINDNESS
BRAILLE
AND THE
BIBLE

BLINDNESS BRAILLE AND THE BIBLE

A CHRISTIAN HOME EDUCATION CURRICULUM

MARY AND JOSEPH STEPHEN

Faithful Generations
South Australia, Australia

ISBN: 978-0-9924875-2-2

This book is for you, my children, to understand better your blind father. May you appreciate what your father had and has to do to achieve things. If your father can achieve great things in spite of his blindness, how much more you who are sighted can do great things for God's glory!

Remember God's standard is very good. (Genesis 1:31)

Remember the Lord Jesus hath done all things well. (Mark 7:37)

Remember God expects the same standard from you. (Ecclesiastes 9:10)

—Mary Florence Stephen

Contents

Acknowledgments

W E WOULD LIKE to thank JT for her tireless and mammoth effort proofreading this manuscript at each typesetting phase, we could not have brought this to publication without your help!

We would like to thank the following blindness organizations and service providers/companies for giving us permission to use their photos:

- Freedom Scientific Inc (www.freedomscientific.com) for photos of note takers, Braille displays, reading machines, and screen-reading software.
- Humanware Inc (www.humanware.com) for photo of the Trekker Breeze hand-held GPS device.
- Quantum: Reading Learning Vision Pty Ltd (www.quantumrlv.com.au) for photo of JotADot, PIAF, and Mountbatten Brailler.
- The Guide Dogs Association of South Australia and Northern Territory (www.guidedogs.org.au) for photos of guide dogs.
- The Guide Horse photo was originally posted to Flickr by DanDee Shots at http://flickr.com/photos/18309730@N00/295965213. It was reviewed at 09:46 on June 9, 2007 (UTC) by the FlickreviewR robot and confirmed to be licensed under the terms of the cc-by-2.0. It is reproduced under the terms of the original poster.
- The Vision Australia Heritage Collection (www.visionaustralia.org) for photo of Louis Braille.
- The Royal Society for the Blind of South Australia (www.rsb.org.au) for photos of white canes.
- All other photos (unless specified) are copyright Mary Florence Stephen.

Chapter 1

Introduction to Blindness

I T IS SAID that the eyes are the window to the soul. This is why many people would rather lose any other sense but their sight. Studying this disability will help you learn empathy and compassion for those on whom the Lord Jesus bestowed such compassion. God gives people with disabilities to families, churches, and communities for this very reason. Learning to serve others with special needs is often the only way we learn to serve without expectation of recompense. We hope after studying this book you'll have more than just a strange curiosity about blindness; we hope you'll have a deep sense of the practical need to help and love people with disabilities. While in developed countries the incidence of blindness is relatively low—about 1.5 percent in Australia—in developing countries this rate is much higher. Every five seconds someone in the world goes blind. Every minute a child goes blind.

More than 75 percent of the world's blindness is preventable. Approximately 90 percent of the world's blind people live in developing countries. More than 83 percent of blind people are over the age of fifty—the majority of blindness is caused through age related issues.[1]

In simple terms, blindness means that someone does not have sufficient sight to walk without guidance or aid. Far more prevalent, however, are people with low vision. Low vision means a person has about a third of the sight or field range of a fully sighted person.

There are varying degrees and kinds of blindness. Not all blind people see nothing. Some see light and dark, some are just color blind, some can only see out the sides of their eyes (peripheral vision), and to some seeing is like looking through a drinking straw (tunnel vision). Some see well at night and bright light hurts their eyes (photophobia), while some see well in bright light but can't function in the dark. Many low vision people are able to make use of the sight they have by using strong glasses, correct lighting, or powerful magnifying aids.

Some people's eyesight will never improve, no matter the lighting, the power of the magnifier, or the contrast of the images. We call someone with an eye condition that makes them legally blind "vision impaired"—rather than *visually* impaired—because their vision is impaired, not their visual appearance. Legal blindness usually means a person has less than 10 percent functional vision. Put simply, what a fully sighted person can see 60 meters away, a legally blind person only can see six meters away.

The "Stick" or White Cane

You may have seen a person walking around with a short, white stick that doesn't reach the ground. This is known as a "symbol cane" and is a sign to onlookers that this person has low vision. A symbol cane serves no other purpose than as a symbol to alert others to the person's low vision condition.

A white cane that reaches the ground is a functioning tool for a person whose vision impairment renders him or her unable to walk around safely without an orientation aid. The white cane alerts users of changes in ground surface and contour, helps them find obstacles before they trip over them and holes that might cause them to stumble, and generally enables them to walk confidently without fear of injury. The white cane is often used to locate landmarks that aid the user in navigating a route from Point A to Point B. The white cane contains no electronic components. The ball you may see on the end of some canes is to stop the cane from sticking in cracks in the ground and injuring the blind person, who if walking at a reasonable pace could easily jab himself or herself in a painful area or break or bend the cane. Many blind people now use folding canes that break into several segments and are held together by strong elastic or fold telescopically like a radio antenna.

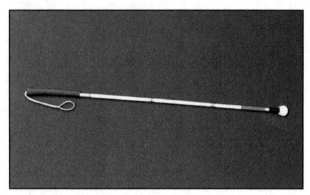

Foldable White Cane Extended

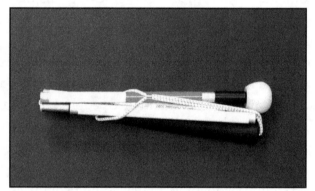

White Cane Folded in Four Segments

When you wait on a two-sided train platform and a train arrives, the sound can be deceiving. Due to the hollow space under some platforms, the sound might travel under the platform and appear to be coming from in front of the waiting blind passenger rather than behind him or her where the train has just pulled in on the other side of the platform, especially if the blind person is sitting in a shelter on the platform with a wall behind him or her. The cane can be used to test if the train is beyond the edge of the platform and to find the door for safe embarkation. I know a blind man who fell off a platform because of this kind of situation. He managed to crawl under the platform to avoid an oncoming train on the track he had just fallen onto.

Guide Dogs

Some blind people prefer to use a guide dog to help them get around. Not all breeds of dog are suitable to be guide dogs, and not all puppies that receive training become guide dogs. Dogs must be even-tempered, trustworthy, instantly obedient, healthy, and able to be suitably trained. Some breeds that have proven suitable include Labradors, German Shepherds, Golden Retrievers, and Labradoodles. The

Labradoodle is a cross between a Labrador and Poodle and is popular amongst those who are allergic to dog fur as the Labradoodle has hair rather than fur.

A guide dog must go through rigorous training. Even after the training is complete, the blind person must ensure that the dog remains obedient at all times. A dog and its potential owner must also complete training together before the dog is able to lead the blind person.

A guide dog might learn the route to familiar places but the blind person is the one giving the dog commands rather than passively following where the dog thinks is best. The blind person is also responsible for telling the dog when it is safe to cross a road, although the dog might refuse to walk if it senses danger that the blind person appears not to realize.

Remember, a guide dog is not a "blind dog" as many people like to call them. But they are also known as "seeing eye" dogs. In recent years, even miniature horses have been used as guide animals.

A guide dog wears a harness with a handle when it is working. The blind person holds the handle and asks the dog to follow different commands such as "forward", "stop", "find the bus" and "find the seat". If the guide dog comes to a kerb or steps, it stops, which lets the person know they have come to an obstacle. If the person is walking towards something they might bump into, the dog guides them around the obstacle.

It is important not to pat or talk to a working guide dog even if the dog is sitting or lying down because it might not be able to concentrate on keeping the blind person safe. Feel free to talk to the person using the guide dog.

Note the sneakers. These have become more and more accepted by guide-horse users as horseshoes tend to set off metal detectors at airports.

Just like sighted people, blind people have varying degrees of confidence and navigational ability. Some love being out and appear very much at ease, while others prefer to go out with other people and are less confident alone. Some prefer to use a guide dog and others, like me, prefer only to use a cane. Concentration and careful use of their other senses are paramount. Crossing a road is obviously very dangerous when there is lots of traffic around, but a windy day can make crossing even a quiet street a nerve-racking experience for the less confident. Modern cars with quiet engines also make pedestrian travel a real challenge for blind people.

Sleep Patterns

It is often—though not always—true that blind people have problems sleeping. This is particularly true for totally blind people whose metabolism cannot be corrected by sunlight. In such cases, blind people may have great difficulty sleeping at night not because of the time but simply because they aren't ready to sleep. The lack of light perception doesn't regulate their body in the same way the absence of light regulates a sighted person's body. I personally have great difficulty sleeping at night even when my body or mind is exhausted. Of course, other factors also affect a blind person's ability to easily fall asleep, such as level of mental activity. Unless a blind person gets into an unbroken and uninterrupted night routine, nighttimes can be a challenge, especially if he or she feels like sleeping during the day instead of at night when everyone else sleeps.

My totally blind friend used to wake up at 3:00 AM to go for his daily walk. He did not expect much traffic around at that time and his body clock was suited to this routine. One day he was tragically killed by a motorist who also did not expect a blind person to be crossing a main road at such a time. This terrible accident highlights the need for both blind and sighted people alike to always be vigilant, even in the middle of the night.

When You Meet a Blind Person

Many people are uncomfortable when they meet a blind person. The following suggestions will help you feel at ease with blind people, and are based on thoughtful courtesies you might extend to anyone, sighted or blind.

- There are many ways in which you can be helpful to blind people in everyday situations, but always ask if they want to be assisted. If help is needed, they'll be grateful. If not, they will thank you for asking. Never grab them by the hand or clothing, or push them along with your hand on the back of their neck.

- Speaking upon entering a room where there is a blind person is very helpful. Identify yourself and those with you and let them know when you're leaving. Don't just exit without informing them and leave them talking to nobody. Also, if after talking to you there is a pause, they might not know if you are still there, so give some kind of indication or they might assume you have left and walked away.

- When greeting a blind person while others are present, use a name or provide some cue so the blind person can tell whom you're talking to. They aren't rude when they don't answer if they don't know to whom you are talking. Also, if a blind person is there when you are greeting someone else, use a name so that the blind person is not embarrassed by answering when you are not speaking to him or her. Remember that blind people can't see when you're looking at them.

- Address a blind person directly, not through someone else, and use a normal tone of voice. Once when I was at a hair salon, the stylist asked my wife, "Would the boy like a drink?" She was referring of course to me, a grown (albeit short) man.

- When giving directions to blind people, be specific. Pointing will not help, nor will "over there." Phrases such as "do you see what I mean" or "let's look at the numbers" are a normal part of everyday conversation, so you needn't censor your conversation. Remember, too, that nods and shrugs do not take the place of words.

- If the blind person chooses to accept assistance when moving through an environment, it will be easiest for him or her to hold onto your arm just above the elbow when walking. This will position you about a half-step ahead, and the individual easily can follow your movements. Walk at a natural pace and pause briefly before ascending or descending steps, and inform the individual whether he or she is going up or down. Don't just say "steps" because the person doesn't know whether to step up or step down. If you do this, the blind person might step up and then fall heavily because he or she is supposed to be stepping down, or try to step down and trip if it is actually a step up.

- When providing assistance to cross the street, stay with the person until the opposite curb has been safely reached. When approaching a step or curb, try to approach it straight on (90 degrees to the step) rather than at an angle, which could cause the person to trip.

- Don't pat, feed, or talk to a guide dog without asking. The dog is a working animal responsible for leading a person who cannot see and should not be distracted or treated like a pet.

- When escorting a blind person to a chair, place his or her hand on the back of the chair, or if approaching from the front, guide the individual to a position where he or she can contact the chair with his or her leg. Be careful that you position the person to sit in the middle of the chair so he or she doesn't fall off the side of the chair. If you take a blind person to a car or bus, guide his or her hands to the door handle and allow the person to manage the rest.

- When you dine with a blind person it can be helpful to describe the table setting. The location of food servings can be described as numerals on a clock face: "Your mashed potatoes are at seven o'clock."

- Always inform blind people if their glass has been refilled or placed in front of them, so they do not accidentally knock it over not knowing it is there. If serving a hot drink, it is very helpful to place the person's hand on the mug handle if sitting at a table. If attempting to give a hot drink to a blind person while he or she is standing, be extra careful you don't take the person by surprise or he or she may jump and knock the hot drink, causing it to spill. As you approach the blind person, warn him or her that you have a hot drink and give instructions on safely taking the mug from you.

- If blind people don't know where food is, they must eat whatever lands on their fork or spoon, even if it is something they'd rather leave or eat with something else on the plate. Such simple things are taken for granted by a sighted person. If you are in a situation where people must serve themselves—such as at a church luncheon—always ask blind people if you may serve them and be sure to be sensible about the amount and kind of food you give them. Always ask if there is something they would prefer to have or not have. If there is finger food, be sure to grab them paper towels on which to wipe their fingers. Remember, their fingers are their eyes, so while it might be easy for you to go wash your hands at a convenient time, it is not so simple for blind people. On the subject of eating, I've had unkind people play tricks on me as I was eating by continuing to pile food on my plate as if it were a bottomless plate, or worse still, mix a dessert and a main course on the same plate. My wife has observed the children of blind people shaking generous amounts of pepper and salt on their blind parent's food as their parent stood talking to others. This underscores the sin nature in us all and highlights the need for vigilance by other adults to deal swiftly with such inappropriate behavior.

- If you have a money transaction, identify the denomination of the bills so the blind person can fold them according to the individual's own method for identification.

- Never grab a blind person's cane to lead him or her—this would be like putting blinkers on sighted people or preventing them from turning their heads to see something. Also, if you see a blind person with a cane heading for an obstacle such as a pole or a wall, never pull them away or force them to change direction unless there is danger. If in doubt, let them know what they're heading for. In many cases they may be looking for the object as their landmark and point of reference. When traveling alone, blind people usually walk from landmark to landmark and must physically contact the landmark to get their bearings.

- If you are leading blind people who are taller than you, make sure you do not walk them under tree branches or beams they may hit, but you miss. Tell them they are approaching a low branch and slow down in time for them to stop before hitting it. When I was much younger, my little brother led me under a low iron-roofed cubby house. He only stopped when he couldn't pull me any farther as the roof had cut into my nose and stuck in it.

- When leading blind people into a room, take them to a place where they can get their bearings rather than just leaving them at a random spot in the room. For example, lead them to a chair, a pole, or a person with whom they are familiar.

- Don't be afraid to tell blind people gently to stop what they're doing or alert them that something is inappropriate. They can't read body language—such as when they bring up a topic you don't wish to discuss—and they are unable to be sensitive to dangerous or inappropriate situations. All the dirty looks and cues to stop will go over their head. Similarly, give cues if they are unsure, such as, "Go on, I'm listening." If they stop talking abruptly, it may be because they think you walked away.

- Because blind people are often unaware of how sighted people act and can't moderate their visual posture based on the surrounding norms, they often have strange habits such as putting their hand or fist in their eye, rocking, moving their head left and right as they talk, dropping their head down, and so on. Feel free to remind them when they are doing such things—sometimes they've had help breaking such habits by thoughtful family or friends but other times these habits have been let go for so long that they still need constant reminding. If you do remind them, do it discreetly so as not to humiliate them.

- If you see blind people waiting in an airport transit terminal, or on a plane as people are disembarking, it is always helpful to ask them if they need help. I've been assisted in airports before, but I've also been left to wait for hours without the courtesy of the assistant returning to see if I need anything while waiting. A blind lady was recently locked in an airplane waiting for promised assistance from ground staff who never came back to help her.

- The most important things you need when meeting blind people are your goodwill and your common sense. Remember that blind people think, feel, and make decisions just as you do. A blind person is an individual who has usually lost only one sense—the sense of sight. Be natural and enjoy one another.

Myths of Blindness

- It is not generally true that blind people like to feel your face. I'll never forget going to a camp one time when an enthusiastic guy came up to me—the first time he'd ever seen a blind person—and excitedly asked, "Do you want to feel my face?" I did it for the fun of it but it is not something I ever think about. Sighted people think like sighted people; blind people only occasionally wonder what things or people look like, and only when it is relevant to their world. For the most part, we forget we live in a visual world until we are faced with a situation requiring visual analysis.

- It is not generally true that blind people have better hearing than sighted people, although they do learn to make better use of this sense.

- Not all blind people wear dark glasses. Those who do may do so because the light hurts their eyes, or for cosmetic reasons such as to hide a prosthetic eye.

- Not all blind people like or use guide dogs.

Embarrassing Situations

I've gone out many times with odd socks, odd shoes, and unmatched clothes. I've accidentally sat on people's laps, fallen in deep trenches while carrying loads of books and school equipment, gotten really lost in familiar places, been caught talking to nobody as the person I had been talking to had long gone, walked into the wrong restroom, and much more. Of course, many of these things happen much less now that I have a wife and children to keep me in line.

Another blind friend once told me how when he was desperate to relieve his bladder he tried to find a tree he thought was well hidden, only to emerge to the cheers of a group of onlookers. That private tree wasn't so private after all.

It's Not Always Serious

While blindness is certainly difficult, there are the occasional funny things that happen. My friend was at the cinema with his guide dog when a lady approached him with a very serious question.

She asked, "Excuse me, but why do you bring your guide dog to the cinema?"

My quick-thinking blind friend responded with his usual quick sense of humor. "Well, you don't think I'd let him go to the cinema alone, do you?"

Speaking of guide dogs, when I used to work with other blind people, my sighted wife caught some guide dogs misbehaving just like children several times. They'd creep away from their owners, go say hello to her, and look at her pitifully for food. Or they would play in quiet wrestling matches while their owners were distracted. One time they got in trouble because in their wrestling frenzy they pulled out a network cable and brought down the department's computer network!

Exercise 1

Circle the most appropriate answer below.

1. How should you lead blind people?

    A. Take them by the hand.

    B. Put your hand on the back of their neck and guide them.

    C. Allow them to hold you just above the elbow.

    D. Grab the end of their cane and lead them.

    E. Call their guide dog to follow you.

2. When you see blind people heading toward an obstacle with a white cane, should you:

    A. Grab them to prevent them from hitting the obstacle?

    B. Allow them to find the obstacle with their cane (unless it is dangerous)?

    C. Gently steer them around the obstacle?

    D. Call out to them that they are about to hit something?

    E. Do nothing?

3. When talking to blind people you should:

    A. Speak extra loudly.

    B. Speak to their companion rather than them.

    C. Introduce yourself by name and talk naturally, and gently touch them on the shoulder if they do not realize you are talking to them.

    D. Never speak to them while they are walking.

    E. Speak to their guide dog instead of them.

4. If you need to leave while a blind person is talking with you, you should:

    A. Politely excuse yourself.

    B. Just walk away.

    C. Wait until he or she is finished speaking and then walk away.

5. When dining with blind people you should:

   A. Ask if they'd like you to describe where their food is, using a clock face for reference.

   B. Just proceed to eat as normal.

   C. Never fill their glass until they ask

   D. Cut up their food for them without asking.

   E. Keep piling food on their plate so they don't go hungry later.

6. When approaching stairs while guiding blind people, you should:

   A. Look for an elevator instead of trying to negotiate stairs.

   B. Stop at the stairs, inform them that there are ascending or descending stairs, and place their hand on the handrail.

   C. Proceed as usual, announcing "steps."

   D. Attempt to carry them down the stairs.

   E. Don't take them to places with stairs.

7. Blind people:

   A. Always see nothing at all.

   B. Always see darkness.

   C. Have varying amounts of sight from nothing to reasonable vision, depending on their eye condition.

   D. Always need to wear dark glasses.

   E. Always use a guide dog.

   F. Always use a white cane.

   G. Always like to feel your face to identify you.

8. If a blind person appears to stop talking to you it may be because:

   A. He or she thinks you have gone away and so needs reassurance you're still there.

   B. His or her eyes hurt.

   C. The person is just rude (some blind people have some strange habits).

9. When entering a room where a blind person is, you should:

   A. Announce your presence and announce who is with you.

   B. Announce your presence.

   C. Say nothing (not drawing attention to his or her blindness).

10. How can you help blind parents?

   A. Keep an eye on their children for them and alert them if the children are doing something inappropriate.

   B. Tell their spouse how sorry you are for them.

   C. Be sensitive to the needs of both the blind and sighted parent. The sighted parent will have an extra responsibility and burden to ensure that both the blind spouse and children are taken care of.

   D. All of the above.

Chapter 2

Personal Testimony and Poems

The Blind Boy

Francis L. Hawks, D.D.[2]

It was a blessed summer day:
  The flowers bloom'd, the air was mild,
The little birds pour'd forth their lay,
  And ev'ry thing in nature smil'd.

In pleasant thought, I wander'd on
  Beneath the deep wood's ample shade,
Till suddenly I came upon
  Two children who had thither stray'd.

Just at an aged beech-tree's foot,
  A little boy and girl reclin'd:
His hand in hers she kindly put,
  And then I saw the boy was blind.

The children knew not I was near;
  A tree conceal'd me from their view,
But all they said, I well could hear,
  And I could see all they might do.

"Dear Mary," said the poor blind boy.
  "That little bird sings very long:
Say, do you see him in his joy,
  And is he pretty as his song?"

"Yes, Edward, yes," replied the maid,
 "I see the bird on yonder tree."
The poor boy sigh'd and gently said,
 "Sister, I wish that I could see."

"The flowers you say, are very fair,
 And bright green leaves are on the trees,
And pretty birds are singing there:
 How beautiful, for one who sees!"

"Yet I, the fragrant flowers can smell,
 And I can feel the green leaf's shade,
And I can hear the notes that swell
 From these dear birds that God has made.

"So, Sister, God to me is kind.
 Though sight, alas! He has not given:
But tell me: are there any blind,
 Among the children up in Heaven?"

"No, dearest Edward; there all see:
 But why ask me a thing so odd?"
"Oh Mary! He's so good to me,
 I thought, I'd like to look at GOD."

Ere long, disease his hand had laid,
 On that dear boy, so meek, so mild:
His widow'd mother wept and pray'd
 That God would spare her sightless child.

He felt her warm tears on his face,
 And said: "oh never weep for me:
I'm going to a bright, bright place,
 Where, Mary says, I God shall see.

"And you'll come there: dear Mary too.
 But mother! when you get up there,
Tell Edward, mother, that tis you,
 You know I never saw you here."

He spake no more, but sweetly smil'd,
 Until the final blow was given;
When God took up that poor blind child,
 And open'd first his eyes in Heaven.

O Love That Wilt Not Let Me Go

George Matheson (1842-1906)

If there is one thing I'd like to communicate through this book, it is the side of blindness not communicated through the media—the difficulty and pain of a disability's effects. One person who knew this all too well was George Matheson, the writer of the painfully meaningful hymn, "O Love That Wilt Not Let Me Go." This was the only hymn Matheson wrote, but its depth eclipses many which are churned out of the modern "Christian worship" factories of today.

He wrote the hymn on the eve of his sister's wedding. His whole family had gone to the wedding and had left him alone. He wrote of something that had happened to him that caused immense mental anguish. Years before, he had been engaged until his fiancée learned that he was going blind and there was nothing the doctors could do. She told him she could not go through life with a blind man.

Matheson went blind while studying for the ministry. His sister had taken care of him, but now she was leaving with her new husband. Matheson was a brilliant student—some say if he hadn't gone blind he could have been the leader of the Church of Scotland. He wrote a learned work on German theology and then wrote *The Growth of The Spirit of Christianity*, a brilliant book according to Louis Benson but with some major mistakes in it. When critics pointed out the mistakes and charged Matheson with being an inaccurate student, he was heartbroken. One of his friends wrote, "When he saw that for the purposes of scholarship his blindness was a fatal hindrance, he withdrew from the field—not without pangs, but finally."

So Matheson turned to the pastoral ministry, and the Lord richly blessed him, finally bringing him to a church where he regularly preached to more than fifteen hundred people each week. But he was only able to do that because of his sister's care, and now she was married and gone. Who would care for him, a blind man? Not only that, but his sister's marriage brought a fresh reminder of his own heartbreak over his fiancée's refusal to "go through life with a blind man."

It was in the midst of this circumstance and intense sadness that the Lord gave him this hymn—written, he said, in five minutes![3]

O Love That Wilt Not Let Me Go

Words: George Matheson
Music: Albert L. Peace

Free Sheet Music from HymnSite.com

O Love that wilt not let me go,
    I rest my weary soul in thee;
I give thee back the life I owe,
    That in thine ocean depths its flow
May richer, fuller be.

    O light that followest all my way,
I yield my flickering torch to thee;
    My heart restores its borrowed ray,
That in thy sunshine's blaze its day
    May brighter, fairer be.

O Joy that seekest me through pain,
    I cannot close my heart to thee;
I trace the rainbow through the rain,
    And feel the promise is not vain,
That morn shall tearless be.

O Cross that liftest up my head,
    I dare not ask to fly from thee;
I lay in dust life's glory dead,
    And from the ground there blossoms red
Life that shall endless be.

Blindness

Joseph Stephen
(From *More than Meets the Eye—Vision in Verse*, ©2009-2010 Joseph Stephen)

It's not that I want sympathy,
    But I do want understanding.
Being blind has many difficulties,
    Especially for a family!

I can't zip up to the shop,
    when we unexpectedly run out of milk.
I can't kick a ball with the children
    Or take them to the park.[1]

I can't bandage a bleeding finger
    or see the extent of a wound.
I can't watch cooking on the stove,[2]
    or catch a baby falling to the ground.

I can't drop my wife off,
    when the carpark is too full,
and drive the children around,
    till she's finished buying food.

She can't drop me off,
    at an unfamiliar stall,
or ask me to find a table,
    in a crowded food mall.

Yes, there are lots of things I can do
    But I can't do so much more.
They don't balance each other out
    Don't reason with me that way.

My dear wife and children
    work overtime to compensate my eyes
My five-year-old leads me round the hardware store
    My wife has no choice but to drive.

---

[1] When children are very young, unless the park has a fence around it, one needs to be careful that the children don't run toward a road, go near the edge of an unsafe piece of equipment, walk in front of a swing, etc. With older children this is not as difficult but it is impossible to do this safely alone, especially if there are other children at the park. Blind people cannot always orchestrate their environment to be exactly how they need it to be to function.

[2] While a totally blind person can cook, taking over the cooking in the middle of the task is not so easy since the blind person usually relies on timing to know how near something is to being cooked. Sighted people don't generally care about timing because they can see that something is cooked. Also, it's not so bad if when living by yourself, you occasionally might have half raw meat—but you don't want to serve this to little children.

Your offers of help are appreciated.
    Please follow through with your pledge.
It's better if you see what needs doing
    To relieve the tension and edge.

Don't get me wrong, I'm not complaining.
    There are many people worse off than us.
I'm writing this as education
    Because things aren't always obvious.

I'm writing so you know how my wife feels,
    So you know how tired she gets.
Everything depends on her eyes,
    It fills life with stress.

Yes, I can change nappies,
    I can cook and bathe the children.
Yes, I can make wooden toys,
    Play hide-and-seek and hug them.

This is not about what I can do,
    For these things I don't need help.
It's to educate and explain what is hard,
    which make life so difficult.

When you're blind things take longer:
    Going shopping, finding a toilet,
Reading the mail, paying the bills,
    Cleaning up the house and garden,
Cooking the meals.

I don't need more advice,
    I'm not asking for a solution.
I'm explaining things so you can understand,
    To reduce people's expectation.

Being blind is hard, there's no doubt,
    Especially with a family!
Please try and remember our plight,
    We need your understanding.

True Vision Does Not Require Eyes

Joseph K. Stephen

When I was born, I had about 2 percent vision in my right eye. While this doesn't sound like much, it was enough to walk around without a white cane and not bang into any obstacles. I lost this 2 percent vision by the time I reached my teen years.

My left eye has always seen nothing at all—not darkness or blackness, but nothingness. My right eye now sees what my brain recreates or imagines should be seen. For example, if I look out a window, my brain imagines what might be out the window and creates a picture of the scenery that would be seen through my right eye. It is only when I go to touch what I think I can see that I realize I can't actually trust what my brain says my right eye sees.

Of course what I think I can see is not at all what a sighted person sees. If I look at a tree, I see a mass of green with no definition or detail. When I look at a person, I see a tall shape, again with no definition or detail. When I look at a doorway, I see a dark area of the wall, but when I go to touch the frame, I realize what I see has no connection to reality and that it is simply my imagination creating a picture of what my brain imagines is in front of me. The shapes and blobs I think I see, however, still help me make some sense of the world around me. Some days I can really tell when the light is on or off and other days I can't see any light at all, or I think the light is on when it is actually pitch black in the room.

Not all blind people have this experience, but it is true that totally blind people who have never seen anything at all out of either eye see neither darkness nor blackness. If you want to know what it is like to be totally blind, wave your hand in front of your ear opening and imagine what you see looking out of your ear. Your ear can't see anything at all, of course—that's nothingness, not blackness or darkness. This is what totally blind people who have never had use of their eyes "see."

As a blind person, I can still enjoy the wonder of God's creation. I love the sound of birds, the sound of a gentle flowing stream, the smell of flowers, the feel of the warm sun on my face, and the feel of a newborn baby's soft skin. I love to taste different kinds of foods from around the world. As I mentioned earlier, it is not true that blind people have better hearing than sighted people, though it is true that we often learn to use our other senses more and thus rely more on our hearing to perceive the world around us. Our lack of sight does not impair our ability to think, however.

One of my favorite verses in God's Holy Word is, "And the Lord said unto him, Who hath made man's mouth? or who maketh the dumb, or deaf, or the seeing, or the blind? have not I the Lord?" (Ex. 4:11). This tells me that God sometimes chooses to allow someone to have a disability for His own glory. The blind man in John 9 was born blind for the sole purpose that God would be glorified through the Lord Jesus Christ publicly healing him. The Lord makes this most profound statement, which by His grace I have found to be true—in a spiritual sense—in my own life: "They which see not might see; and that they which see might be made blind" (John 9:39). While I do not see physically, my spiritual eyes have been opened to what many who see with their physical eyes do not see.

While God does not often choose to heal those with a disability today, they are still born to glorify Him through other aspects of their lives. I seek to glorify God through the gifts He has given me.

I count myself extremely blessed not only to have a wonderful wife and eight precious children, but to be employed in a way that helps other blind people. I work as a software engineer, developing screen-reading software to enable blind people to use a computer. Considering that the unemployment rate among blind people is in excess of 70 percent[4], I have much for which to be thankful.

Some of the other opportunities I'm grateful to God for include:

- The opportunity to ride a tandem bicycle from Adelaide to Canberra—a distance of more than 1,400 km—to raise money for the Australian Bible Society
- The opportunity to learn woodwork and make wooden toys for my children
- The enjoyment of being able to cook for my family
- The opportunity to work from home and help with the education of my children
- The ability to publish books
- The privilege of serving the Lord even with a disability

If there is one bit of advice I would give to anyone who is blind or going blind, it would be this: Don't underestimate the impact your blindness will have on your sighted family. We live in an age of political correctness gone mad that leads to an over-emphasis on equal opportunity. This often gives blind people an unrealistic view of their disability. I'm not talking here about what a blind person can or can't achieve, but that we live in a sighted world and regardless of the technology at our disposal, our blindness will always impact others whether we like it or not. Having said that, be strong, aim high, and know that God has allowed your blindness for His glory. Make sure you glorify Him in your weakness.

> And he said unto me, My grace is sufficient for thee: for my strength is made perfect in weakness. Most gladly therefore will I rather glory in my infirmities, that the power of Christ may rest upon me.
>
> —2 Cor. 12:9

Practically speaking, this scripture means there is always someone who is worse off than you and there is always someone better off than you.

> Let your conversation be without covetousness; and be content with such things as ye have: for he hath said, I will never leave thee, nor forsake thee. So that we may boldly say, The Lord is my helper, and I will not fear what man shall do unto me.
>
> —Heb. 13:5-6

Thank You, Lord

Joseph K. Stephen
(From *More than Meets the Eye—Vision in Verse*, ©2009-2010 Joseph Stephen)

Thank You, Lord, for loving me,
    Before I knew You existed.
Thank You, Lord, for saving me,
    The chief of sinners attested.
You give purpose and meaning to everything made,
    Your wisdom is marvelously and richly displayed,
Not a speck in all space can another claim stake,
    Not a second of eternity Your knowledge escape,
How foolish and proud to even consider,
    That without You we possibly could ever be better.

Thank You, Lord, for Your precious Word,
    It is better than infinite treasure.
Thank You, Lord, for Your presence sure,
    That no distance nor peril can sever.
My heart cries out with a yearning so strong,
    To consecrate my life to Lord Jesus alone.
No matter the road or the mountain steep,
    To live by faith and Your commandments keep.
For living life without regard to Your will,
    Is utter futility and totally nil.

Thank You, Lord, for my dear wife,
    For the privilege and honor of marriage.
Thank You, Lord, for my children,
    Each one a blessing so cherished.
My prayer is that all my progeny will,
    Worship, obey, and live faithfully till
With a shout and the voice of the archangel strong,
    The Lord Jesus comes to call us all home.
But till the day of that most glorious sound,
    May I be a man of integrity found.

Thank You, Lord, for my blindness,
    Yes, even this disability.
Thank You, Lord, for each trial,
    You've told me that they are good for me.

For if I had sight, the lust of the eyes,
> Perhaps I'd be damned, Your Word I'd despise.
I know of a truth that all You allow,
> Is for Your purpose though we may not know how.
I accept my lot as Your choicest of ways,
> and render to You the most reverent of praise.

We asked several other blind people to write about living with blindness from a Christian perspective—the challenges, decisions, and difficulties they face as they deal with life.

My View from the "Blind Side"

Stefan Slucki (married, no children)

Before I formed thee in the belly I knew thee; and before thou camest forth out of the womb I sanctified thee, and I ordained thee a prophet unto the nations.

—Jer. 1:5

And I will bring the blind by a way that they knew not; I will lead them in paths that they have not known: I will make darkness light before them, and crooked things straight. These things will I do unto them, and not forsake them.

—Isa. 42:16

For me as a blind person, those two fragments of God's Word are most precious indeed!

I was born with an entirely curable eye condition, glaucoma, which was diagnosed early, so humanly-speaking I ought to be wearing thick glasses and benefiting from 80 percent of vision, but the Sovereign Lord has appointed another path for me.

Since becoming a Christian at age eighteen, I have found the twin truths of security and significance—found in God's call to Jeremiah—of great comfort. They overwhelm any feelings of "why me, Lord?" types of resentment at my being blind, which occasionally do surface.

Discrimination against those with disabilities continues, mostly through ignorance and fear. In my case, my wife and I think it's due to people not being able to make eye-contact with me.

For all believing Christians, however, the promises of Isaiah 42 should be precious! Certainly in a literal sense the Lord sometimes sends kind and helpful people to me when I am lost, but I am so grateful for a good sense of direction and strong health apart from my lack of sight.

My wife, Sue, is fully sighted. She feels pressured when other sighted people expect her to do all the formal things of life that are easier for a sighted person to do but not necessarily easy for every sighted person to do. Obviously, she has to drive everywhere and do many things that only a sighted person can do.

We prayed about these things before we got married, which was a good thing to do, but nothing can fully prepare you for the challenges that arise at times. At such times, personal and joint prayer is the best first step, followed by a discussion on how to tackle the issue.

As James says: "If any of you lack wisdom, let him ask God." (1:5).

So what would help us as a Christian couple? A continued maturing in Christ, of course, and a continued maturing in society that leads to growth in acceptance of blind people as normal, contributing members of society.

Blindness Is a Challenge

Ursula Bennett (married, ten children)

Blindness is a challenge for the spirit. We were created to respond to God's beauty and goodness in worship, much of which we perceive through the eyes. To still adequately respond to God's love in worship, we must make deliberate effort to perceive beauty and love through our other senses, which are challenged in compensation due to lack of visual information intake. This allows for a great opportunity to base our worship response more firmly on the unchanging facts of creation, redemption, and sustenance that exist constantly beyond human sensory perception, and to learn to love God with our minds through memorization of and meditation on God's Word. Concentrating on this is easier due to lack of visual distractions.

Blindness is a challenge for the soul because sometimes our need for independence and creativity is not adequately met. Because the rest of the body is working normally, we expect to be able to perform—especially domestic duties—but it takes us more time and does not provide as much satisfaction as it does for a sighted person. The balance between work and recreation requires more effort to fine tune, posing a great opportunity for deepening relationships between Christian brothers and sisters. Like any other disability, blindness gives the church fellowship the opportunity to show the larger community the outworking of the new commandment the Lord Jesus gave us: to love one another. This love might be adequately expressed between brothers and sisters with all functioning faculties through actions that enhance already functioning life. But the love shown to a blind or otherwise disabled person can make the difference between his or her soul being nourished or stunted, and therefore, I believe it has a great "wow" factor attached to it when the world observes it.

Blindness is a challenge for the body. We must be deliberate about exercise and good nutrition to keep fit and healthy.

Blindness is a challenge for the family. Sometimes our attempts to discipline our children can be misdirected because we do not know all the contributing factors of disobedience. Children are greatly tempted to misrepresent the truth because they know their blind parent is unable to set the record straight. These dynamics between parent and child can also be distorted through the need for children to perform adult duties, such as reading private mail or writing checks. This creates a great opportunity for trust built on the love of truth, the need for which is highlighted in a family where blindness is present, especially in a parent.

The fact that there are difficulties attached to blindness is a great indication that we were created with all faculties working. I am looking forward to the time when all evil is done away with—including blindness. To say I am glad that I am—through the Lord Jesus—able to look forward to heaven is an understatement. It is the hope that keeps me going through this rather unpleasant time of darkness. The Holy Spirit is training me to keep my eyes fixed on my Lord and to, like Him, endure suffering for the joy that is set before me in the promise of eternal life.

Knowing I Would Go Blind

Stephen Greeley (recently married)

I had low vision when I was born—20/400 in my right eye and 20/600 in my left eye. In fact, the doctors could not believe I could see at all. When I was a baby, my mom would put something on a table and I would crawl over and pick it up, so obviously I could see at least a little bit. But doctors could not figure out *how* I could see. I had retina folds, which meant that if I had vision at all I should have had severe tunnel vision. But for twenty-three years God gave me a normal range of peripheral vision. I could see colors and could see well enough to ride a bike, although not well enough to drive.

Since I was five years old I've known I would lose my vision, it was just a matter of when. So when I did lose my vision, it really didn't matter. Why? Because when most people lose their vision later in life it is a big deal, but unlike most people I did not go through any grieving for the loss of my vision.

I grew up in a very loving Christian home. Both my parents knew Christ as their Savior before they were married. From age five to eleven I was in a program at Church called Awana. When I was eight years old my Awana leader asked me if I wanted to accept Christ as my Savior and I said yes but that I wanted to ask my dad to help me do that. So later that night I did ask my dad and I admitted to Christ that I was a sinner. I told Him I believed He was God and the Son of God. I thanked Him for dying on the cross in my place and that I believed He did rise again from the grave. I thanked Him for the free gift of salvation I chose to accept knowing there was nothing I could do on my own to save myself. I told Him I chose to trust in Him alone for my salvation.

Later, when I was nine, I chose to be baptized in the name of Christ. Awana gave me the solid foundation I needed to function for the rest of my life. This is why my favorite verse is "Let your conversation be without covetousness; and be content with such things as ye have: for he hath said, I will never leave thee, nor forsake thee" (Heb. 13:5). Time after time throughout my life God has demonstrated over and over that He loves me and that I can completely rely on Him.

In August 1993, when I was twenty-three, I woke one morning to find everything had turned red and sparkly. Very quickly—in a matter of minutes—I lost the rest of my vision. I've been completely blind since then. I have a little light perception on the periphery but no shape perception. I only see bright white and a bit of blue. I see no other colors except a bit of black and gray. Inside buildings I see nothing at all. Everything is black. So I can tell outside where the sun is and often if the sky is blue or if I see black shapes of a building, but that is all. I could not tell you if I was standing in front of a tree or a person. I do have some perception that something is nearby, but I could not tell you what that might be unless, for example, someone spoke, and then I would know there is a person there.

The reason I did not grieve as most people do when they lose their vision later in life is because I had the Lord to rely on. I simply told God, "Well, Lord, I guess You'll just have to take care of me. Now I don't have any choice at all but to completely rely on You." And that is exactly what He has been doing for me ever since.

In the past, several Bible verses were my favorites. But now Hebrews 13:5 is definitely my favorite. I delight in the fact that the next face I will see is the Lord Jesus' face in heaven. It's an incredible thought. He is truly real and He does do great things and small little things in our lives. Many people ask why we have difficulties in our lives if God loves us. Why do we sometimes get hurt or have financial difficulties, or why do things not seem to go in our favor? The answer is that if everything went well for us all of the time, what reason would we have for involving Him in our lives? What reason would we have to rely on him? What reason would we have for developing a personal relationship with Him? What reason would we have for seeking His counsel and wisdom, or for seeking His comfort or love? He gave us the Holy Spirit as a helper in these things. If all went well, we would probably ignore Him and leave Him out of our lives.

God's timing isn't always what we would like in terms of our own timing. But He knows what is best for us. When you look back at what God has done, you can see the amazing blessings He has granted as well as how He has interacted in your life. If things never went wrong we would not have the opportunity for Him to show us what an incredibly awesome God He is.

For many years I prayed for the Father to bring me a wife who shares the same heart and love for Him, who shares the same life goals, and with whom I could spend the rest of my life. Unbeknownst to me, Jennie, my wife, was similarly asking the Father for the same thing in a husband. In November 2009 God answered that prayer and brought into my life the woman who became my wife. We were married in June 2010, and she is more incredible than I ever could have imagined. I thank God every day for sharing her with me. She and I have the same life goals, we love to do all the same things—we even have the same favorite color—and we both deeply love the Lord and want to serve Him in whatever capacity He allows.

When Jennie and I talk of the things we went through in our past, we can understand why God did not bring us together earlier in our lives. Both of us had some growing up to do and many things we had to learn before we were ready for marriage. But now that we are together, it seems like we've always been together. God helps us both throughout the day.

Chapter 3

His-Story

The Christian Influence on Society for Those with a Disability

BEFORE THE INFLUENCE of Christianity, particularly in the pagan Greco-Roman Empire but also in other cultures, anyone with a disability would have been left to die or would have been murdered at birth.[5] We have Christianity to thank for the compassion bestowed on those with disabilities such as blindness, which has enabled many to achieve what was impossible before. Even Louis Braille's critical contribution only was possible because of his father's Christian faith, which motivated him to teach Louis to read using raised letters, and then to send him away to a school for the blind where he could be helped further. We must keep this in mind in our current culture where euthanasia and abortion are issues against which many Christians seem to be unwilling to speak out. This Christian compassion toward the disabled has been eroded in recent times—we must understand why and reverse this evil trend.

Margaret Sanger, founder of Planned Parenthood[6], was an atheist who spoke for many who do not recognize the intrinsic worth of human life when she said, "Blind, deaf, dumb, mute and epileptics… this dead weight of human waste."[7] Her desire to rid the world of anyone she thought unfit to live or reproduce contributed to the modern abortion, eugenics, and euthanasia movements. Ironically, and tragically, it was a deaf-blind woman by the name of Helen Keller—herself transformed by Anne Sullivan's Christian charity—who became one of Sanger's greatest promoters.[8] Sanger's world view was taught to many Christians and hence shaped attitudes about children in general and the disabled in particular through her promotion of abortion and birth control.

Sanger was not alone in her drive to rid the world of the disabled. She reflected Charles Darwin's diabolical philosophy, who had said, "With savages, the weak in body or mind are soon eliminated; and those that survive commonly exhibit a vigorous state of health. We civilized men, on the other hand, do our utmost to check the process of elimination; we build asylums for the imbecile, the maimed, and the sick; we institute poor-laws; and our medical men exert their utmost skill to save the life of every one to the last moment. There is reason to believe that vaccination has preserved thousands, who from a weak constitution would formerly have succumbed to small pox. Thus the weak members of civilized societies propagate their kind. No one who has attended to the breeding of domestic animals will doubt that this must be highly injurious to the race of man."[9]

Darwin's and Sanger's influential propaganda stand in stark contrast to the Lord Jesus' compassionate attitude and actions: "Who can have compassion on the ignorant, and on them that are out of the way; for that he himself also is compassed with infirmity" (Heb. 5:2). (Also see Matthew 14:14 and 20:34, Mark 1:41 and 3:4, and Luke 6:9.) Darwin and Sanger were acting consistently with their evolutionary world view (survival of the fittest), which affords man no greater status than an animal. We must ensure that as Christians we are consistent to our world view by knowing God's Word and will. It is tragic how inconsistent we Christians can be in our thinking. We must understand every issue of life from God's revealed Word and not from the faulty philosophies of man's godless and pragmatic reasoning.[10]

There is a side to the euthanasia debate that many have not considered: a person's desire to die because others have made that person feel like a burden on society. I have at times felt this overwhelming hopelessness, and it was only through the help of Christians who reminded me of my worth in God's eyes that this depression did not lead to terrible consequences. Certainly in an environment where euthanasia is legal, this becomes a very real and frightening danger to those with a disability, and a temptation to their families or caregivers who are constantly faced with the burden of caring for or tolerating that disability.

Blind people may have a physical disability with very real limitations, but they also have great potential to contribute to society in other ways. While blind people, like sighted people, must develop and use their God-given talents for their Creator's glory, ultimately all of our worth is based on our heavenly Father's declaration that we were created in His image, and not what we can or can't do.[11]

A Brief History of Braille and Assistive Technology

Besides talking about blindness in this book, my wife and I are going to teach you Braille using God's Word, the Holy Bible. Blind people, like sighted people, need to learn to read so—first and foremost—we can read God's Word. God tells us in Proverbs 4:7, "Wisdom is the principal thing; therefore get wisdom: and with all thy getting get understanding."

The Braille Bible is huge! The King James version is eighteen hardbound volumes—fourteen Old Testament and four New Testament. These books take sixty inches of space on a shelf that is twelve inches high and twelve inches deep—about two average-width bookshelves. They weigh just over 64 pounds or 29 kg. Each volume's pages are double-sided with Braille (English Grade Two) embossed on both sides of each page. Each line of dots slightly offset from the line on the reverse side of the page. The current cost to produce each volume is $19 (American dollars) or $342 for a complete Bible. Production is funded by donations—the Braille Bible is free to any vision-impaired person who requests it.

Here is how the books are dispersed in the King James version of the Braille Bible:

OLD TESTAMENT

Volume 1: Genesis and Exodus Chapters 1-11
Volume 2: Exodus Chapters 12-40 and Leviticus
Volume 3: Numbers and Deuteronomy Chapters 1-21
Volume 4: Deuteronomy Chapters 22-34, Joshua and Judges

Volume 5:   Ruth, 1 Samuel and 2 Samuel
Volume 6:   1 Kings and 2 Kings
Volume 7:   1 Chronicles and 2 Chronicles
Volume 8:   Ezra, Nehemiah, Esther and Job
Volume 9:   Psalms
Volume 10: Proverbs, Ecclesiastes and the Song of Solomon
Volume 11: Isaiah
Volume 12: Jeremiah
Volume 13: Lamentations and Ezekiel
Volume 14: Daniel, Hosea, Joel, Amos, Obadiah, Jonah, Micah, Nahum, Habakkuk, Zephaniah, Haggai,
            Zechariah and Malachi

New Testament

Volume 15: Matthew and Mark
Volume 16: Luke and John
Volume 17: Acts, Romans, 1 Corinthians and 2 Corinthians
Volume 18: Galatians, Ephesians, Philippians, Colossians, 1 & 2 Thessalonians, 1 & 2 Timothy, Titus,
            Philemon, Hebrews, James, 1 & 2 Peter, 1, 2 & 3 John, Jude and Revelation

Joseph and his eighteen volume Braille KJV Holy Bible. The year 2011 AD marked the 400th Anniversary of the KJV.

I learned Braille when I was about eight years old. It took several years to learn and many more to become a fluent reader. God used Louis Braille to invent this raised system of dots called "Braille" that blind people use to communicate.

Until recently Braille was a very complex code. For example, a single symbol may have had multiple meanings depending on its context. The symbol ⠢ , for instance, had four meanings.

If preceding a number it was a dollar sign, if preceding letters it was a contraction for the three letters "dis," if in the middle of a word it meant "dd," and if at the end of a word it was a period.

⠢			
Preceding a number	Preceding letters	Middle of a word	End of a word
$	dis	dd	.
e.g. $1	e.g. disappear	e.g. added	e.g. go.

There were many such symbols with multiple meanings determined by context. There also were completely separate codes for mathematics, chemistry, music, English literature, and all the other subjects and languages. With various codes like this, a single print symbol may have had multiple representations in Braille depending on whether you were using English Braille, Maths Braille, or the chemistry code.

The Unified English Braille Code (UEBC) was developed to overcome some of the issues with multiple codes because they even differed between English-speaking countries. UEBC is slowly gaining widespread acceptance, as it makes learning and translation much easier since each symbol has fewer meanings. In UEBC, for instance, the symbol ⠢ now only means either "dis" if at the beginning of a word, or a period or decimal point. Also, the various codes (other than the music code) have all been merged into a single code where each symbol only means that symbol. Rules about spacing of Braille symbols have also been relaxed in UEBC. In this book we will not burden you with the complexity of the old system—we will use only UEBC. For more information on UEBC, go to www.ebility.com/roundtable/aba/ueb.php.

Imagine the challenges a blind person faced before UEBC to learn mathematics, chemistry, physics, etc. I am the only blind person who has studied mathematics and physics at university level in South Australia, and it was indeed a challenge.[1]

Before the Perkins Brailler, Braille had to be embossed by hand using what is known as a slate and stylus. Each dot had to be manually punched from the top of the paper downward. This meant that the person had to punch the Braille dot-by-dot backward from right to left, and then turn over the page to read the dots. So not only did they have to master the complex system of contractions, which used to be more complex than it is now with the UEBC, but they also literally had to know the code backward. Writing Braille backward from right to left was also much slower and error prone since you couldn't read what you had written without taking the page out of the slate frame and turning it over. Then if more had to be brailled, you had to place the page back in the slate frame in the correct position and count the cells in the frame to find the correct location to begin punching again. This was, as you can imagine, very difficult and time consuming.

---

[1] Joseph is the first and (as of 2011) the only totally blind person to complete a Bachelor of Science degree (majoring in computer science) in South Australia. This Braille book will show you how difficult learning English Braille is. Not being proficient in Braille is a barrier for blind people, let alone mastering the subjects in those books. Not only did Joseph have to know English Braille, but also Maths Braille, Physics Braille, Computer Science, and Indonesian Braille. He was also awarded the Golden Key Award for finishing in the top 15 percent of Flinders University graduates the year he graduated.

Embossing Braille by hand using a Slate and Stylus. Braille must be embossed from right to left and back to front so that when the page is turned over, the Braille can be read.

With the invention of the Perkins Brailler and other similar earlier machines, Braille could be embossed an entire cell at a time using typewriter style keys. The Braille could be read immediately since the dots were embossed from under the page upward. Now we have pocket-sized Braille writers such as the JotADot.

Using a Perkins Brailler, a manual Braille Writer.

Left of spacebar from middle to outermost key: dots 1, 2 and 3; right of space bar from middle to outermost: dots 4, 5 and 6.

Today, we also now have what are known as "Braille embossers." These are Braille printers that connect to a computer, much like an ink printer but without ink. Embossers can Braille at a rate between fifteen and fifty characters per second. The Mountbatten Brailler can also be used for direct Braille entry and word processing, having a Braille keyboard and software built-in. Some industrial embossers used for large-scale production can Braille many pages per minute, and some can also Braille graphics.

Software known as a "Braille translator" must be used to turn ordinary word processor documents into Braille to be embossed on an embosser. The documents cannot be brailled without translation. Translation software makes the job of a Braille transcriber much easier, although he or she still needs to know Braille to check the work and proofread what comes out of the embosser.

Using a JotADot, a pocket-sized manual Braille writer.

Using a Mountbatten Brailler, an electric Braille writer and Braille printer (also known as a Braille embosser).

Devices such as the PIAF (Pictures in a Flash) have been invented to create raised diagrams. The diagram is photocopied onto special swell paper that is then fed through the PIAF. The PIAF heats the swell paper and the diagram is raised.

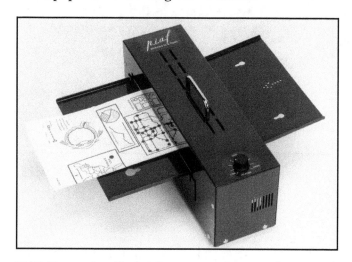

PIAF: Pictures In a Flash – diagrams are drawn or photocopied onto special swell paper and then passed through the PIAF which causes the diagram to be raised, allowing a blind person to feel the diagram.

Other inventions such as the Braille watch or clock, talking watch or clock, talking calculators, talking tape measures, talking kitchen and bathroom scales, talking thermometers, and talking color identification devices are now available to help blind people in their everyday lives.

Hand-held GPS (Global Positioning System) technology is also now available to aid a blind person with mobility. The Trekker Breeze is an example. This incredible device is a hand-held talking GPS system specifically designed for a blind person to use. It works when walking as well as in a moving vehicle. It automatically adjusts the amount of feedback based on the

Braille Watch: The lid of the watch lifts up to allow a blind person to feel the hands and dots on the watch face in order to tell the time.

Talking Scientific Calculator: As the blind person enters mathematical expressions, the calculator speaks the symbols and final result.

speed you are moving. Of course, a GPS device can never replace a person, but it can certainly help blind people to get around by themselves.

Trekker Breeze: This pocket sized talking device uses GPS technology to allow a blind person to navigate around the country unaided.

Special software is available to enable a blind person to use an ordinary computer to do word processing, read and write email, use the Internet, work with spreadsheets and databases, and even program computers. This special software is known as a "screen reader." Many screen readers can also be used to generate Braille, which can be seen on a special Braille display connected to the computer. Braille displays typically have between twenty and eighty Braille cells that change to show the dots of the text on the line at the cursor. With a screen reader, blind people can both hear and feel the text they are editing or reviewing.

Screen reading technology and Braille displays are very expensive. Joseph is one of the programmers who develops the world's leading screen reading technology. He uses his own software to develop his software!

Devices such as the Pacmate Braille note-taker and Pacmate Omni were invented for students or those requiring the convenience of a hand-held device to take notes or manage their work. These are equivalent to a standard PDA except with a Braille or QWERTY keyboard built in. These devices use speech synthesis to speak to the user as well as optionally show the text being edited on a built in or separate Braille display connected to the device.

Today, blind people can even use special software to take a photo of a printed page either using a scanner or camera and within seconds have the computer read the text from the printed page. This powerful software can interpret text in columns or with various fonts and layout. Reading machines such as the SARA CE have been developed for those who want a stand-alone device to read to them rather than having to learn how to use a computer.

The first reading machine was invented in the 1980s and was the size of a washing machine. It cost more than $50,000. Today, software can be loaded onto a mobile phone with a camera to do the same job much more accurately for around a fiftieth of the price. Nothing, however, can replace a kind person reading to his or her blind friend.

You may ask, if Braille is so complex, and blind people can now use talking computers, why learn Braille at all? Braille is a blind person's handwriting. There are times when computers and other technology such as an audio recorder are unavailable or unreliable so being able to take notes by writing and reading Braille is essential.

Also, some subjects are spatial in nature and are impossible to study in an audio fashion. Have you ever tried to do long division in your head or in audio? You would find it very difficult because of the way the brain works. The same part of your brain that processes audio also processes math, wheras the part of the brain that interprets print or Braille is separate, making reading and processing much easier than listening and processing. Also, when laying out figures you need to refer to the intermediate results you've already calculated, something that is almost impossible without print or Braille. Some subject matters such as tables of figures, accounts, and so on are almost meaningless when read aloud so having them in Braille is essential.

When presenting information in a lecture or conference, a blind person can't easily refer to audio notes while speaking, so it is essential to have notes or an outline in Braille. While audio labels are now available, Braille labels are more versatile and useful, especially when locating items in a noisy environment.

Another factor is cost: computers and appropriate software are far more expensive than a simple hand frame or manual Braille writer. Many blind people still prefer to read Braille on paper than to listen to audio or read Braille from a computer. When you use a computer for almost every other task, sometimes it is just good to get away from it.

Focus 80 Braille Display: This is a refreshable Braille display with 80 cells, one of the largest available. This allows a blind person to read longer lines of text without having to pan to read more text on the same line. An 80 cell Braille Display is very expensive, typically in excess of $10,000.

Focus 40 Blue Braille Display: This blue-tooth refreshable Braille display allows a blind person to read Braille output from a computer or mobile phone screen.

SARA CE: The Scanning and Reading Apparatus, Camera Edition, takes a picture of a page and within a few seconds, reads it to the blind user in a human sounding voice.

Mother and son using Pacmate PDA: The Pacmate is the world's first talking PDA with optional Braille keyboard and display which runs standard pocket PC applications.

Louis Braille

Louis Braille was born in France on January 4, 1809. When Louis was three years old he injured his eye with a sharp tool while unsupervised in his father's workshop. This injury eventually caused

his total blindness. Even though Louis went blind, his father did not give up trying to find new ways for helping Louis to read. Initially he created a system of raised letters that were difficult to replicate. Books using this system were large, cumbersome, and very slow to read.

When Louis was only fifteen he invented his system of raised dots, which was later called "Braille" in his honor. This system was made up of a six-dot cell like this. Because the six dots fit under a fingertip, reading with this system was much faster than the raised letters Braille's father had used. Louis initially developed a code for writing music before he developed his literary code.

Louis's injury is an example of what the Apostle Paul meant when he wrote, "And we know that all things work together for good to them that love God, to them who are the called according to his purpose" (Rom. 8:28). While Louis's injury was unpleasant, God used his life to help

The year 2009 AD marked the 200th anniversary since the providential birth of Louis Braille.

blind people everywhere. As Louis Braille lay dying of tuberculosis, he said, "God was pleased to hold before my eyes the dazzling splendors of eternal hope. After that, doesn't it seem that nothing more could keep me bound to the earth?" He died on January 6, 1852, at age 43.

Abraham Nemeth

Blind scientist Abraham Nemeth earned the title "Einstein of the sightless" for inventing the first Braille code of mathematics. Born into a dedicated Orthodox Jewish home, Nemeth as a boy soaked up biblical and Talmudic lore by listening to his grandfather hour after hour. It was not until 1950 that the Jewish Braille Institute of America, working with rabbinical groups abroad, completed the standard Hebrew-language edition of the Scriptures for blind readers. Abraham Nemeth paid a debt of love to his grandfather's memory by serving as proofreader for the world's first Hebrew Braille Bible.[12]

Nemeth said, "One of my grandfathers was particularly attentive to me, and he gave me the religious training that I now possess. He would try to find messages that would be encouraging to me and that would serve as a guide for me as a blind person. One of those messages, which has stayed with me and which has had particular impact on me during all the years that I was growing up and by which I am still guided, is: 'It is better to light a candle than to curse the dark.'"[13]

David Madison Spencer

David was the son of David Spencer and Dorcas Tabitha Rose, the youngest of nine children. He was born April 1, 1855, in Ravanna, Mercer County, Missouri, and he died March 26, 1923, in Missouri. He printed what may have been the first American Braille Bible.

Spencer's occupation was "blind preacher." However, he is listed in the 1880 Worth County, Missouri, census as a "book agent."

Spencer was hit in the left eye by a sickle. He was taken to Indianapolis, Indiana, for treatment but after ten days returned home totally blind for life. He lived with his family until his mother died in 1872, and then he was placed into a school for the blind in St. Louis, Missouri. There he learned to read Braille, which increased his desire to one day write the first Braille Bible in America (prior to that they had only been printed in France). His father died shortly after his returning home from this blind school. That winter, under the earnest efforts of Elder A.C. Long, he was converted and came under the Lordship of Christ, and sought Him to be his life companion to guide him through a life of darkness. With the advice of friends and the aid of a young boy to drive him in his horse-drawn wagon, he sold books, preached, and spent his spare time working on the Braille Bible. He later said it took him seven years to complete.[14]

David Spencer, Louis Braille, and Abraham Nemeth contributed immensely to the world of the blind, motivated by their deep love for and awe of God, their Creator.

Chapter 4

Learning Braille

UNLIKE PRINT, WHICH comes in a multitude of sizes and shapes, production Braille is typically a single size. This size is optimal to fit under the fingertips used for reading. There is such a thing as jumbo Braille, where the dots in the six-dot cell are spaced farther apart and the dots themselves are larger, but this is typically only used to help teach children who have multiple disabilities, such as a learning disability or problems with finger sensitivity.

Throughout this book, we've used a Braille font approximately the same size as production Braille. We've used two different Braille fonts, one with a shadow to show dot patterns within their context in the six dot cell, and in exercises beyond 7.2, we've removed the shadow dots to make the dot patterns look more like production Braille.

Some readers may have already been introduced to the Braille alphabet during their education. Use of the Braille alphabet alone with no other contractions is known as Grade 1 Braille. Most blind readers learn Grade 2 Braille (which is what we are teaching in this book). Grade 2 adds many abbreviations and other symbols to make the language more compact. This reduces the size of Braille volumes which are already much larger than print volumes of equivalent text. Since we are teaching Braille gradually, the most appropriate dot patterns for certain word signs will not be used until you have been introduced to them. We'll start off learning Grade 1 and introduce new symbols as we go along. By the end of the book you'll know the most appropriate dot patterns to use for most words.

Lesson 1: The Braille Cell

In the Braille cell, the dots are numbered as follows:

```
1 ● ● 4
2 ● ● 5
3 ● ● 6
```

The left column from top to bottom is made up of dots 1, 2, and 3.

The right column from top to bottom is made up of dots 4, 5, and 6.

For example:

> "a" = dot 1
> "b" = dots 1 and 2
> "c" = dots 1 and 4

Definitions

1. Simple sign—a sign occupying one cell only
2. Composite sign—a sign occupying two or more cells
3. Upper sign—a sign containing dot 1, or dot 4, or both
4. Lower sign—a sign containing neither dot 1 nor dot 4
5. Contraction—a sign that represents a word or a group of letters
6. Groupsign—a contraction that represents a group of letters
7. Wordsign—a contraction that represents a whole word
8. Shortform—a contraction consisting of a word specially abbreviated in Braille.[1]

---

[1] Unified English Braille Primer; Australian Edition; Editor: J. Howse; Preliminary Edition 2006; Page 10.

Braille Alphabet

Here is the Braille alphabet:

a	b	c	d	e	f	g	h	i	j
⠁	⠃	⠉	⠙	⠑	⠋	⠛	⠓	⠊	⠚

k	l	m	n	o	p	q	r	s	t
⠅	⠇	⠍	⠝	⠕	⠏	⠟	⠗	⠎	⠞

u	v	w	x	y	z
⠥	⠧	⠺	⠭	⠽	⠵

Notice how the letters "a" through "j" look very similar to the letters "k" through "t", except they also have dot 3 in the cell?

Can you spot the odd letter out?

Hint: "u" looks like "a" with dots 3 and 6 in the cell, and "z" looks like "e" with dots 3 and 6 in the cell.

If you said "w" you are correct. "W" was added later because the French do not use the letter "w." Below, "w" is separated out. See if you can spot the similarities between the letters:

a	b	c	d	e	f	g	h	i	j
⠁	⠃	⠉	⠙	⠑	⠋	⠛	⠓	⠊	⠚

k	l	m	n	o	p	q	r	s	t
⠅	⠇	⠍	⠝	⠕	⠏	⠟	⠗	⠎	⠞

u	v	x	y	z
⠥	⠧	⠭	⠽	⠵

w
⠺

EXERCISE 1.1

a	b	c	d	e	f	g	h	i	j

Memorize the Braille letters above by dot numbers and patterns as you transcribe the following words:

EXERCISE 1.2

k	l	m	n	o	p	q	r	s	t

Transcribe the following words using letters "a" to "t."

⠉⠓⠊⠇⠙⠗⠑⠝ ⠍⠁⠙⠑ ⠎⠑⠁⠞ ⠚⠑⠎⠞ ⠛⠕⠕⠙

⠎⠕⠕⠝ ⠍⠁⠏ ⠃⠗⠊⠙⠑ ⠗⠕⠙ ⠕⠁⠞⠎ ⠋⠕⠝⠙

⠇⠕⠁⠙ ⠎⠝⠁⠏ ⠛⠇⠁⠙ ⠗⠕⠉⠅ ⠍⠑ ⠞⠊⠏

⠞⠁⠅⠑ ⠝⠕⠙ ⠗⠊⠏⠑ ⠎⠑⠑ ⠇⠑⠞ ⠎⠕⠁⠏

⠗⠕⠁⠙ ⠍⠑⠑⠞ ⠎⠁⠍⠑ ⠎⠁⠇⠑ ⠇⠁⠍⠑

⠍⠕⠎⠎ ⠏⠕⠇⠇ ⠝⠕⠎⠑ ⠗⠁⠞⠞⠇⠑ ⠉⠕⠍⠍⠁⠝⠙

⠍⠑⠞⠁⠇ ⠋⠇⠕⠁⠞ ⠊⠝⠎⠏⠊⠗⠑ ⠃⠕⠗⠝ ⠁⠛⠁⠊⠝

⠊⠍⠏⠕⠗⠞⠁⠝⠞ ⠓⠕⠍⠑ ⠁⠃⠇⠑ ⠞⠕⠍⠃ ⠓⠁⠍

⠅⠑⠞⠞⠇⠑ ⠍⠁⠝ ⠉⠁⠍⠏ ⠛⠕⠇⠙ ⠃⠊⠗⠙ ⠗⠕⠇⠑

⠚⠁⠍⠎ ⠃⠁⠝⠛ ⠋⠕⠇⠙ ⠍⠊⠗⠑ ⠁⠝⠊⠍⠁⠇

⠁⠎⠅ ⠎⠑⠑⠅ ⠅⠝⠕⠉⠅ ⠞⠓⠁⠝⠅

EXERCISE 1.3

u v w x y z

Using letters "a" to "z," transcribe the words below.

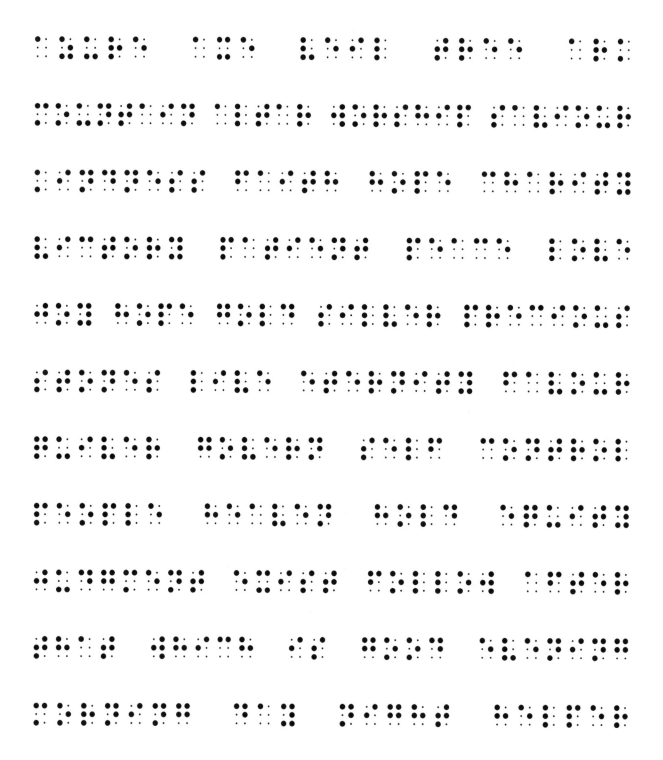

Lesson 2: Braille Numbers

The numbers 1 through 0 are the same as the letters "a" through "j" except that we add a number sign ⠼ prior to the first letter as follows:

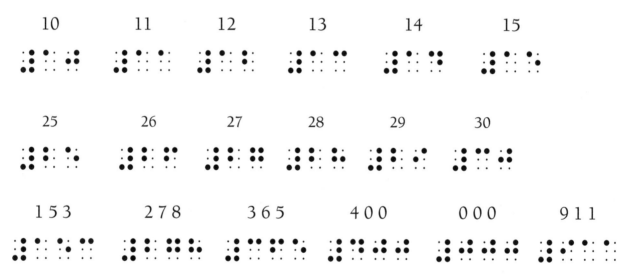

Examples:

10   11   12   13   14   15

25   26   27   28   29   30

153   278   365   400   000   911

Exercise 2.1

Transcribe these Braille numbers. Write your answers underneath the Braille numbers.

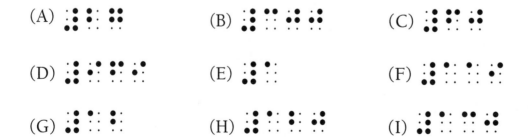

(A)   (B)   (C)

(D)   (E)   (F)

(G)   (H)   (I)

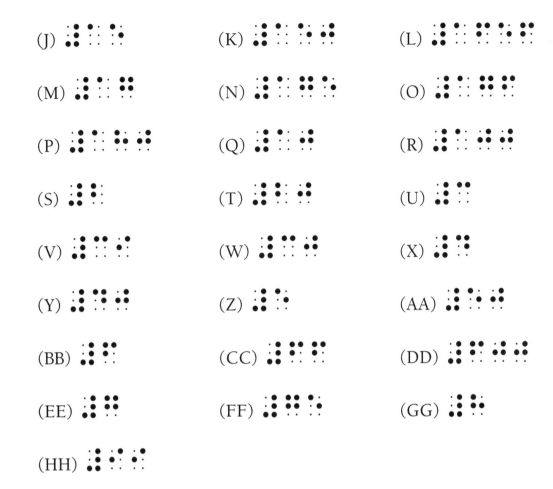

(J)　(K)　(L)

(M)　(N)　(O)

(P)　(Q)　(R)

(S)　(T)　(U)

(V)　(W)　(X)

(Y)　(Z)　(AA)

(BB)　(CC)　(DD)

(EE)　(FF)　(GG)

(HH)

Exercise 2.2

Use the Braille numbers you transcribed in Exercise 2.1 and insert the corresponding number in the boxes.

Example:

(a) Books in the Bible: (CC)

Answer: (CC) in Braille is the number 66.

(a) Books in the Bible: (CC)

(b) Books in the Old Testament: _____

(c) Books in the New Testament: _____

(d) On day _____ of creation, God divided the light from the darkness.

On day _____ of creation, God made the sky.

On day _____ of creation, God made land and sea, and all plants.

On day _____ of creation, God made the sun, moon, and stars.

On day _____ of creation, God made sea creatures and birds.

On day _____ of creation, God made land animals and man.

On day _____ of creation, God rested from all His work.

(e) And all the days of Methuselah were _____ years.

(f) From creation to flood took _____ years

(g) Noah was commanded to build an ark _____ cubits long by _____ cubits high by _____ cubits wide. There was _____ window in it _____ cubit from the top. There were _____ stories.

(h) Noah was commanded to bring _____ of each clean animal and _____ of each unclean animal into the ark.

(i) Noah had _____ sons.

(j) There were _____ people on the ark.

(k) It rained for _____ days. The waters were _____ cubits above the tallest mountain.

(l) The waters prevailed upon the earth for _____ days. The ark rested in the _____th month, on the _____th day of the month, upon the mountains of Ararat.

(m) The waters decreased continually until the _____th month; in the _____th month, on the _____st day of the month, the tops of the mountains could be seen.

(n) Noah waited another _____ days before he let a raven and a dove go out the window.

(o) After the dove returned, he waited another _____ days and let the dove go again.

(p) After the dove returned with an olive leaf, Noah waited yet another _____ days.

(q) In the _____th and _____st year, in the _____st month, the _____st day of the month, the waters were dried up from off the earth: and Noah removed the covering of the ark, and looked, and, behold, the face of the ground was dry. (Gen. 8:13)

(r) In the _____nd month, on the _____ and _____th day of the month, was the earth dried.

(s) Abraham had Isaac when he was _____ years old and Sarah was _____.

(t) Isaac married Rebekah when he was _____ years old.

(u) Jacob was born when Isaac was _____ years old.

(v) Abraham died when he was _____ years old.

(w) When Abraham died, Isaac was _____ and Jacob was _____.

Jacob had _____ sons and _____ daughters (that we know of).

Isaac died at _____ years old. When he died, Jacob was _____ years old.

(x) Jacob was _____ years old when he stood before Pharaoh. He died soon after that.

(y) There were _____ apostles.

(z) There are _____ Psalms and the longest is _____ with _____ verses.

Lesson 3: Capitalization

Capital Sign

To capitalize a letter, we add a dot 6 before the letter like this:

G   o   d

L o r d   J e s u s   C h r i s t

To capitalize the whole word, we add two dot sixes before the word.

H O L Y   B I B L E

L O R D

EXERCISE 3.1

Transcribe the Braille words according to the capitalization rules.

Jeremiah 9:23 and 24

     saith the   ,   not the wise man glory in his wisdom, neither let the mighty man glory in his might, let not the rich man glory in his riches:

     let him that glorieth glory in this, that he understandeth and knoweth me, that   am the   which exercise lovingkindness, judgment, and righteousness, in the earth: for in these things   delight, saith the   .

EXERCISE 3.2

Translate using Grade 1 Braille (without any Braille contractions) and without Braille punctuation. (Literary punctuation has been used instead since you have not learned Braille punctuation yet.)

EXERCISE 3.3

See if you can transcribe the following verse. This time, literary punctuation has been removed, and the Braille font is more challenging because it doesn't have the shadow for the other cells.

Lesson 4: Contractions

Contractions are dot combinations devised to help make Braille more compact since Braille is larger than the print in regular books.

Wordsign: A contraction that represents a whole word

Here are five of the most common symbols:

and	for	of	the	with
⠯	⠿	⠷	⠮	⠾

EXERCISE 4.1

Transcribe the following using the common contractions for "and," "for," "of," "the," and "with."

Revelation 4:11

Thou art worthy, O Lord, to receive glory ⠯ honor ⠯ power; ⠿ thou hast created all things, ⠿ ⠿ thy pleasure they were, ⠯ are created.

Mark 8:38

Whosoever therefore shall be ashamed ⠷ me ⠯ ⠯ my words in this adulterous ⠯ sinful generation; ⠷ him also shall ⠮ Son ⠷ man be ashamed, when he cometh in ⠮ glory ⠷ his Father ⠯ ⠯ holy angels.

Luke 12:8

Also I say unto you, Whosoever shall confess me before men, him shall ⠮ Son ⠷ man also confess before ⠮ angels ⠷ God:

Lesson 5: Simple Upper Wordsigns

Most alphabet letters are used to represent a whole word when they stand alone (preceded and followed by a space or punctuation). They are called "simple upper wordsigns" because the Braille letter has at least one dot on the top line of the cell.

a	b	c	d	e	f	g
a	but	can	do	every	from	go

h	i	j	k	l	m	n
have	i	just	knowledge	like	more	not

o	p	q	r	s	t	u
o	people	quite	rather	so	that	us

v	w	x	y	z
very	will	it	you	as

b	but	c	can	d	do	e	every		
f	from	g	go	h	have	j	just		
k	knowledge	l	like	m	more	n	not		
p	people	q	quite	r	rather	s	so		
t	that	u	us	v	very	w	will		
x	it	y	you	z	as				

Examples:

You cannot use "just" to represent "just" in "unjust" because the "j" does not stand alone.

just   unjust

EXERCISE 5.1

Look for the capital letter sign, contractions, and uncontracted words. Punctuation has been removed except for the literary colon in the verse reference.

⠰⠎⠀⠨⠑⠀⠒⠀⠨⠁

⠰⠎⠀⠰⠃⠀⠃⠀⠰⠺⠑⠀⠺⠑⠀⠺⠑⠀⠰⠃

⠺⠑⠺⠑⠀⠃⠀⠰⠉⠀⠺⠑⠀⠺⠑⠀⠰⠉

⠺⠉⠺⠑⠀⠃⠀⠰⠉⠀⠃⠀⠺⠑⠺⠀⠃

⠺⠑⠺⠑⠀⠺⠑⠺⠑⠀⠃⠀⠃⠀⠺⠑⠺⠀⠃

⠃⠑

⠰⠃⠀⠰⠑⠀⠰⠃⠀⠒⠀⠰⠁

⠺⠑⠺⠑⠀⠃⠀⠺⠑⠀⠺⠑⠀⠃⠀⠃⠀⠺⠑⠺

⠃⠀⠺⠑⠺⠀⠃⠀⠺⠑⠀⠺⠑⠺⠑⠀⠺⠑

⠺⠑⠺⠑⠀⠃⠀⠺⠑⠺⠀⠺⠑⠀⠺⠑⠀⠃

⠃⠑⠀⠰⠑

Lesson 6: Punctuation

Description	Print	Braille
Period or Full Stop	.	⠲
Comma	,	⠂
Question mark	?	⠦
Exclamation	!	⠖
Colon	:	⠒
Semicolon	;	⠆
Apostrophe	'	⠄
Left quote	"	⠦
Right quote	"	⠴

Note that the question mark and left quote look similar, however you can tell from the context which it is because you do not precede a word with a question mark in English.

EXERCISE 6.1

Transcribe the following Braille full stop, comma, colon, and semi-colon.

Psalm 127

1. A Song of degrees for Solomon ⠒ Except the Lord build the house ⠆ they labour in vain that build it ⠒ except the LORD keep the city ⠆ the watchman waketh but in vain ⠲

2. It is vain for you to rise up early ⠆ to sit up late ⠆ to eat the bread of sorrows ⠒ for so he giveth his beloved sleep ⠲

3. Lo ⠆ children are an heritage of the LORD ⠒ and the fruit of the womb is his reward ⠲

4. As arrows are in the hand of a mighty man ⠆ so are children of the youth ⠲

5. Happy is the man that hath his quiver full of them ⠒ they shall not be ashamed ⠆ but they shall speak with the enemies in the gate ⠲

EXERCISE 6.2

Transcribe the following Braille full stop, comma, exclamation, question mark, apostrophe, left quote, and right quote.

The prophet Amos said ⠦ ⠦ Hate the evil and love the good ⠐⠔ ⠦ God hates evil ⠖ The Lord ⠄ s mercy is toward them that fear him ⠲ Do you fear the Lord ⠦

Lesson 7: Wordsigns - Using Dot 5 and a to y

The dot 5 wordsigns may also be used as a contraction within a word.

Example: <u>understanding</u>

Simple Wordsign			Initial Wordsign			
	1871	1905			1905	1932
c	Christ	can	Dot 5 and	c	Christ	omitted
d		do	Dot 5 and	d	day	
e		every	Dot 5 and	e	ever	
f		from	Dot 5 and	f	father	
g	God	go	Dot 5 and	g	God	omitted
h		have	Dot 5 and	h	here	
j	Jesus	just	Dot 5 and	j	Jesus	omitted
k		knowledge	Dot 5 and	k	know	
l	Lord	like	Dot 5 and	l	lord	
m		more	Dot 5 and	m	mother	
n		not	Dot 5 and	n	name	
o		o	Dot 5 and	o	one	
p		people	Dot 5 and	p	part	
q		quite	Dot 5 and	q	question	
r		rather	Dot 5 and	r	right	
s		so	Dot 5 and	s	some	
t		that	Dot 5 and	t	time	
u		us	Dot 5 and	u	under	
w		will	Dot 5 and	w	work	
y		you	Dot 5 and	y	young	

Important history note:

As we learned earlier, Louis Braille was a Christian. This was later reflected in the original choice of English wordsigns. In circa 1870, "c" for "Christ," "g" for "God," "l" for "Lord" and "j" for "Jesus" were originally part of the simple wordsigns because these words were in common use. This was at the height of the 1817 revival in Australia when the most common discussion in the pages of the *Sydney Gazette* was the merits of Bible reading.[15]

In 1905, these four contractions were transferred to dot 5 and c, dot 5 and g, dot 5 and l, and dot 5 and j (to reflect their declining usage). (Originally, capital letters were not distinguished in Braille. The capital sign, dot six, was only introduced after 1905.) In 1932, dot 5 and c, dot 5 and g, and dot 5 and j were removed from the standard code altogether.[16]

The removal of these signs reflects the decline of Christianity in Britain and the rest of the world as part of the atheist agenda to remove any reference to Jesus, Christ, or God. Even though "Lord" is used to address God, dot 5 and l for "Lord" remains in the standard code presumably because of the continuing existence of British nobility. Throughout the remainder of this book, we will continue to use three contractions—dot 5 and j for Jesus, dot 5 and c for Christ, and dot 5 and g for God—in honor of Louis Braille and to the glory of God.

You can only use the "ever" contraction when the stress is on the first "e" and the "ever" is not preceded by an "i" or an "e". For example, "clever," "never," "sever," and "reverent," may all use the "ever" contraction. Words such as "believer," "retriever," "reverberate," "revere," etc., cannot use the "ever" contraction because these words break these rules. "Everybody" and other words containing "every" are brailled using the "ever" contraction followed by a "y." The simple wordsign for "every" ("e" on its own) may not be used when joined to other letters.

The "here" contraction may only be used when it forms a single syllable and is not followed by the letters "d," "n," or "r." (In these cases, the contractions for "ed," "en," and "er" must be used.) The following are legal uses: "adhere," "herewith," "hereto," "sphere." Illegal uses: "adhered," "inherent," "heresy" (in "heresy," the "here" does not form a single syllable).

The contractions for "day," "father," "know," "lord," and "mother" may be used wherever the letters they represent occur, even where they do not maintain their meaning. All of the following examples are legal uses: "days," "Monday," "daybreak," "Faraday," "fatherhood," "unfatherly," "knowing," "unknown."

The word "acknowledge" must use the "dot 5 and k" contraction since the single letter "k" for "knowledge" may only be used when standing alone or with punctuation, like other single-letter abbreviations.

The following words all use the dot 5 contractions: "overlord," "lording," and "motherly," "mother-in-law," but the word "chemotherapy" does not use the "dot 5 and m" contraction. Instead, it uses the "the" contraction.

EXERCISE 7.1

Transcribe the following verses first using the dot 5 and "c" to "y" initial wordsign. (Note: To simplify this first exercise, only standalone words using the dot 5 contraction should be translated.)

Proverbs 23:17—Let not thine heart envy sinners: but be thou in the fear of the ⠿⠿⠿⠿ all the ⠿⠿ long.

Proverbs 12:19—The lip of truth shall be established for ⠿⠿ but a lying tongue is but for a moment.

Mark 6:3—Is not this the carpenter, the son of Mary, the brother of James, and Joses, and of Juda, and Simon? and are not his sisters ⠿⠿ with us? And they were offended at him.

Proverbs 4:1—Hear, ye children, the instruction of a ⠿⠿, and attend to ⠿⠿ understanding.

Proverbs 18:10—The ⠿⠿ of the ⠿⠿⠿⠿ is a strong tower: the righteous runneth into it, and is safe.

Proverbs 15:12—A scorner loveth not ⠿⠿ that reproveth him: neither will he go unto the wise.

1 Peter 4:14—If ye be reproached for the ⠿⠿ of ⠿⠿⠿, happy are ye; for the spirit of glory and of ⠿⠿⠿ resteth upon you: on their ⠿⠿ he is evil spoken of, but on your ⠿⠿ he is glorified.

1 Corinthians 10:27—If any of them that believe not bid you to a feast, and ye be disposed to go; whatsoever is set before you, eat, asking no ⠿⠿ for conscience sake.

Proverbs 4:16—For they sleep not, except they have done mischief; and their sleep is taken away, unless they cause ⠆⠢ ⠒⠖ to fall.

Proverbs 25:19—Confidence in an unfaithful man in ⠐⠄ ⠲⠆ of trouble is like a broken tooth, and a foot out of joint.

Proverbs 12:24—The hand of the diligent shall bear rule: but the slothful shall be ⠐⠄ ⠲⠔ tribute.

Proverbs 20:11—Even a child is known by his doings, whether his ⠐⠄ ⠲⠆ be pure, and whether it be ⠒⠖ ⠲⠄.

Proverbs 30:17—The eye that mocketh at his ⠐⠄ ⠲⠖, and despiseth to obey his ⠐⠄ ⠲⠖, the ravens of the valley shall pick it out, and the ⠆⠢ ⠒⠖ eagles shall eat it.

EXERCISE 7.2

Now transcribe the previous verses according to the Braille rules learned so far. From now on, the Braille font used will not have the shadow.

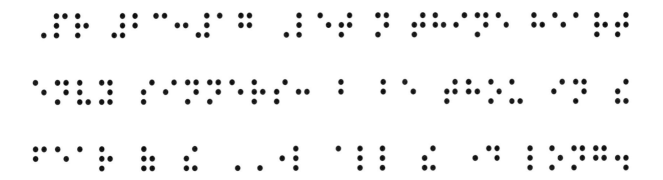

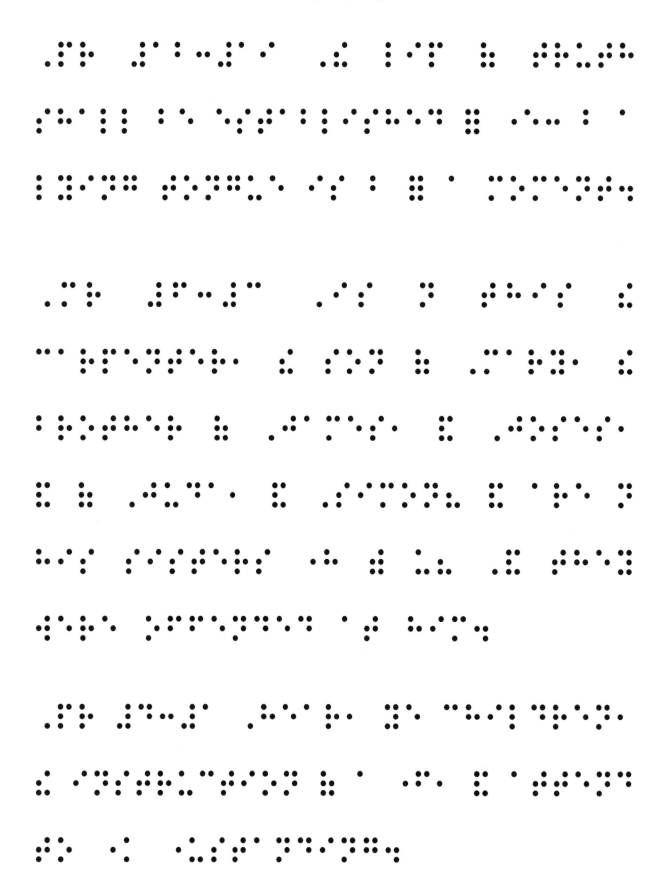

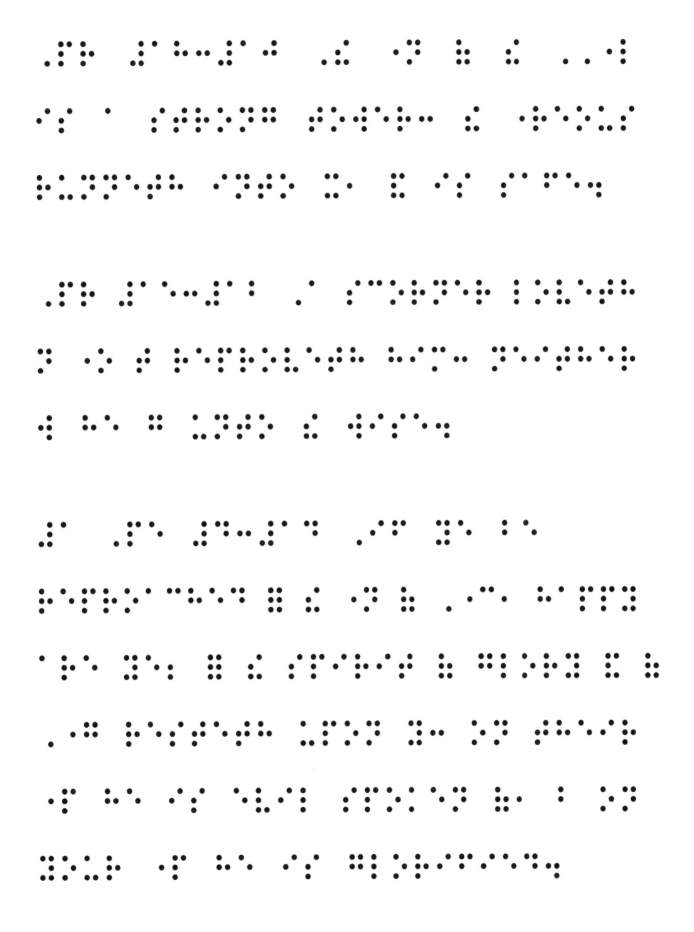

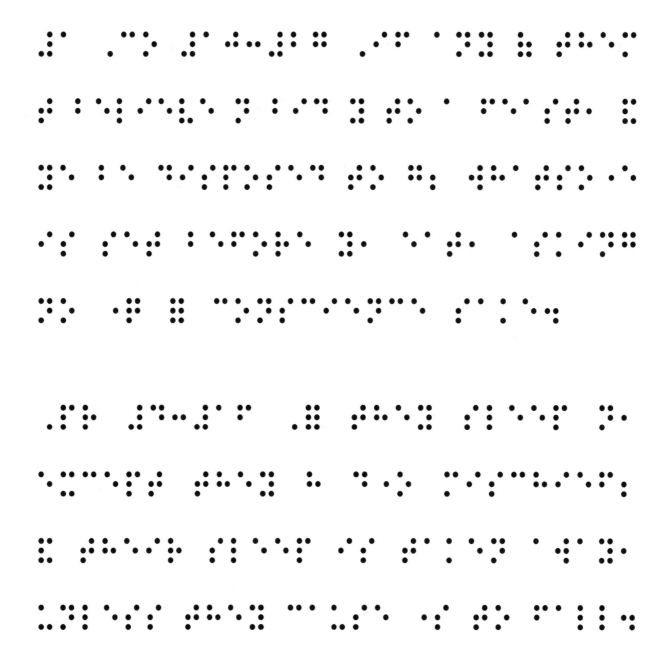

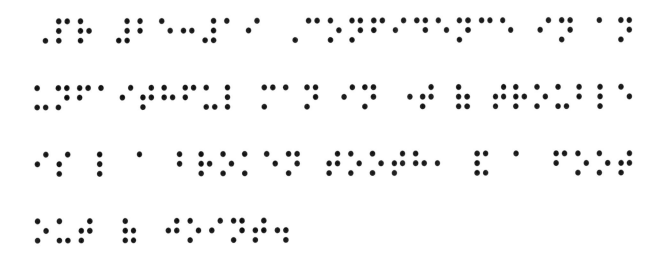

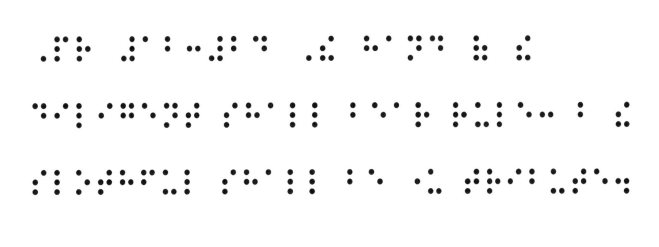

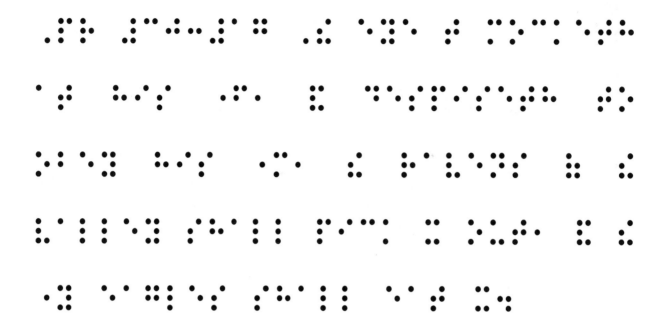

Lesson 8: Simple Upper Groupsigns—and, for, of, the, with

Groupsign—a contraction that represents a group of letters.

and	for	of	the	with
⠯	⠿	⠷	⠮	⠾

You were already introduced to these signs in an earlier section as standalone signs, but these signs can also be used as contractions to form part of a word. However, the "of" contraction may only be used when the "o" and "f" are in the same syllable. For example, "soft," "lofty," "often," but not "profane."

Examples:

hand	forgive	lofty	they	wither

EXERCISE 8.1

Transcribe the Braille contractions using the above groupsigns.

Psalm 127:4—As arrows *are* in ⠿ ⠮ ⠾ ⠾ a mighty man; so *are* children ⠾ ⠮ youth.

Psalm 86:5— ⠮ ⠾ thou, Lord, *art* good, ⠮ ready to ⠾⠿⠷⠮⠯⠿ ⠾ plenteous in mercy unto all ⠾ ⠮ that call upon ⠾ ⠮.

Psalm 131:1—A Song ⠷ degrees ⠷ David. LORD, my heart is not haughty, nor mine eyes ⠿⠾⠯⠮: neither do I exercise myself in great matters, or in things too high ⠯ me.

Psalm 2:12—Kiss ⠮ Son, lest he be angry, ⠾ ye perish *from* ⠮ way, when his wrath is kindled but a little. Blessed *are* all ⠮ ⠾ that put ⠾ ⠯ ⠾ trust in him.

Psalm 1:3— ⠿ ⠿ he shall be like a tree planted by ⠿ rivers ⠿ water, that bringeth ⠿ ⠿ ⠿

his fruit in his season; his leaf also shall not ⠿ ⠿ ⠿; ⠿ whatsoever he doeth shall prosper.

Upper Groupsigns: Dot 6 and a to i

These nine contractions are formed by adding dot 6 to the alphabet signs for a, b, c, d, e, f, g, h, and i.

ch	gh	sh	th	wh	ed	er	ou	ow
⠡	⠣	⠩	⠹	⠱	⠫	⠻	⠳	⠪

These signs can be used in any part of a word.

charity   taught   shalt   saveth

whole   wedding   servant   thou   sow

When a word contains the letters "thed" or "ther," use the groupsign "the" rather than the groupsigns "th," "ed," or "er". For example: "cathedral further."

EXERCISE 8.2

Transcribe the following according to the Braille rules learned thus far.

Note: Because we are introducing contractions bit by bit, some words in the earlier exercises may not have been contracted in the most appropriate way. For example, in Exercise 8.2, the word "such" uses the "ch" contraction because that was already introduced; however, there is a shorter way of contracting this word that will be explained in a later section. Please do not get confused as these are introduced bit by bit—by the end of the book you will know the best way of contracting most words.

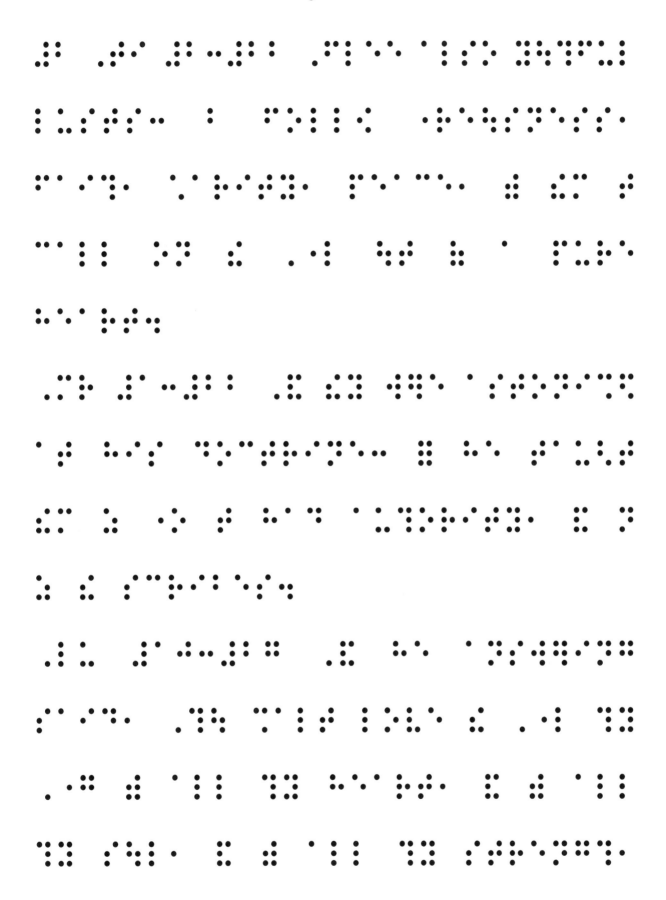

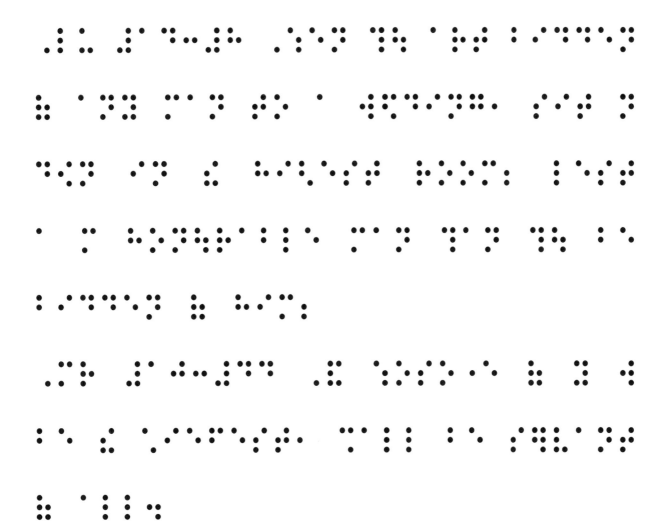

Lesson 9: Wordsigns - ch, sh, th, ou, wh

"ch," "sh," "th," "ou," and "wh" are also used as wordsigns when they stand alone or with punctuation:

ch   stands for "child"

sh   stands for "shall"

th   stands for "this"

ou   stands for "out"

wh   stands for "which"

As we saw with the simple upper wordsigns (such as "k" for knowledge; "p" for people), they may only be used to express the exact word they represent and when no other letters are added to them.

Example:

Pr 23:24 The father of the righteous shall greatly rejoice: and he that begetteth a wise child shall have joy of him.

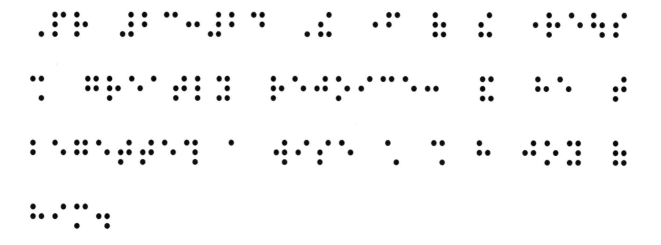

EXERCISE 9.1

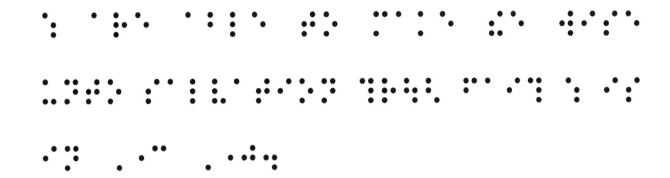

EXERCISE 9.2

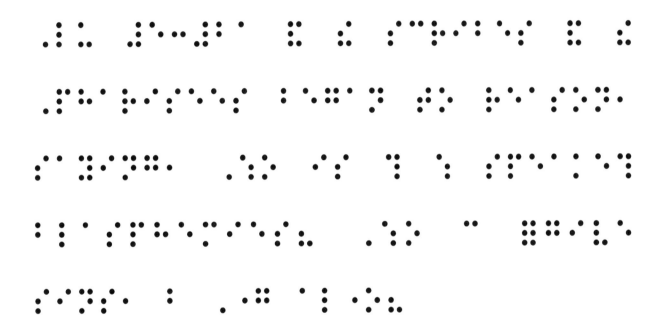

EXERCISE 9.3

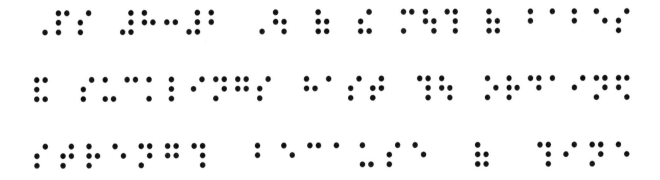

EXERCISE 9.4

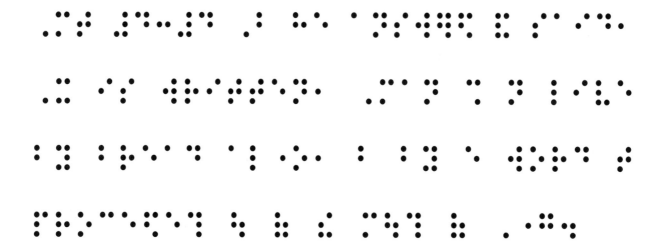

Lesson 10: Upper Wordsigns - Dot 5 and ch, th, wh

Dot 5 and ch	character	⠐⠡
Dot 5 and th	through	⠐⠹
Dot 5 and wh	where	⠐⠱

These signs can be used to form larger words as long as the sign forms a natural syllable, e.g. "any<u>where</u>" ⠁⠝⠽⠐⠱; "<u>throughly</u>" ⠐⠹⠇⠽

Example:

Ephesians 2:8—For by grace are ye saved ⠐⠹ faith; and that not of yourselves: it is the gift of God:.

Proverbs 29:18— ⠐⠱ there is no vision, the people perish: but he that keepeth the law, happy is he.

2 Timothy 3:17—That the man of God may be perfect, ⠐⠹⠇⠽ furnished unto all good works.

Exercise 10.1

Note: The word "rather" has its own contraction, which you have learned. So instead of using the symbol for "the" (⠮) in "rather" (⠗⠁⠮⠗), we use the letter (⠗) which represent "rather" (⠗) on its own. However, the word "these" has its own contraction but because it has not been taught yet, we will just use the symbol for "the" (⠮) in "these" (⠮⠎⠑). Also, the symbols for dash (-) and left and right parentheses () have not been introduced yet so the literary symbols have been left as they are.

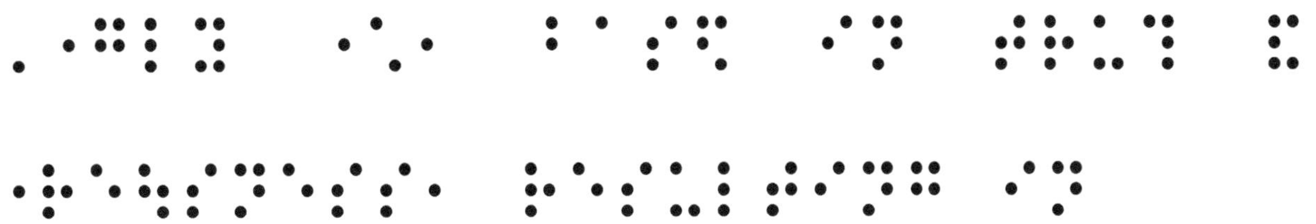

Lesson 11: Upper Wordsigns - Dot 5 and ou, w, y, the

Dot 5 and ou	ought	⠐⠳
Dot 5 and w	work	⠐⠺
Dot 5 and y	young	⠐⠽
Dot 5 and the	there	⠐⠮

The wordsign "ought" may be used as a groupsign wherever the letters it represents occur, regardless of pronunciation (e.g. th<u>ought</u>, dr<u>ought</u>,).

The others in this group retain their meaning when used as groupsigns, i.e. as part of a longer word (e.g. <u>work</u>man, <u>young</u>er, <u>there</u>fore).

EXERCISE 11.1

Note: There is a Braille contraction for "these" but since we have not learned it yet, we will just use "the" in th<u>ese</u> (⠮⠎⠑). Also we haven't learned the contraction for "your" so we will just use the Braille contraction "ou" in y<u>our</u> (⠽⠳⠗). "Their" and "these" are represented by a Braille contraction respectively. For "their" we will just use the Braille contraction "the" in th<u>eir</u> (⠮⠊⠗) and for "these" we will use "the" (⠮⠎⠑).

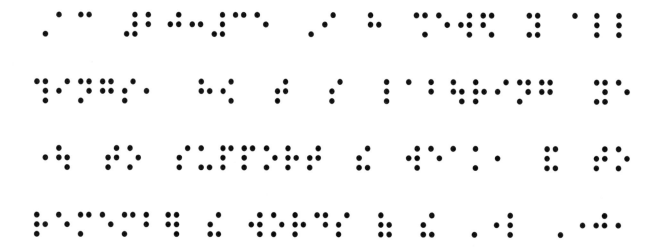

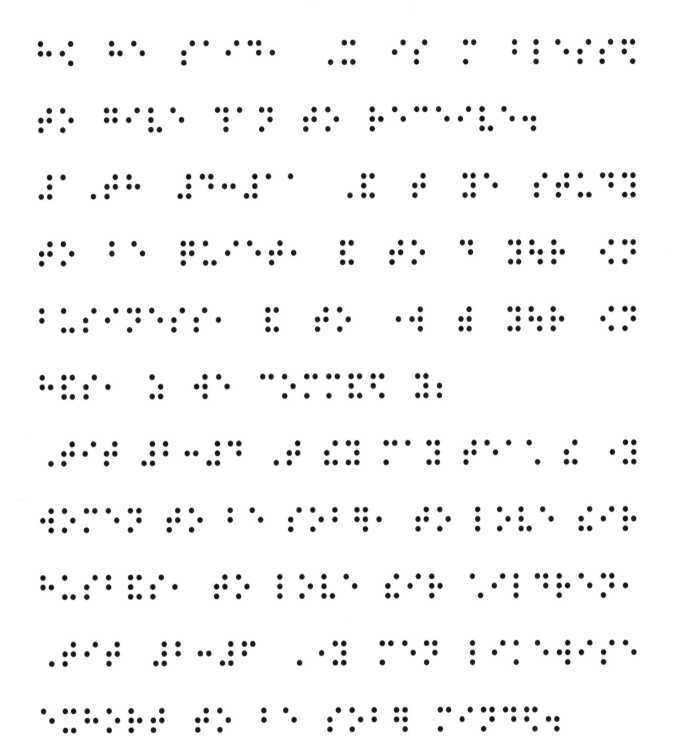

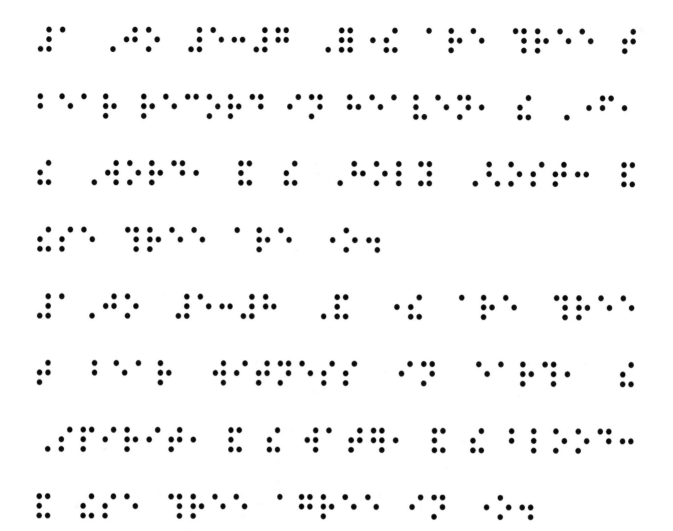

Lesson 12: Last Three Upper Groupsigns - st, ar, ing

st	dots 3 and 4	⠌
ar	dots 3 and 4 5	⠜
ing	dots 3 and 4 6	⠬

Wordsign: "St" by itself stands for the word "still." The same rules on its use as a wordsign apply as in "ch" for "child," "ou" for "out," etc.

The "ing" sign may be used in any part of a word except at the beginning.

Always use the groupsigns that represent the greatest number of letters. For example, in the word "there" there are several possibilities—the "th" sign, the "the" sign, and the "there" sign. You always use the contraction that represents the greatest number of letters unless that contraction spans a syllable boundary, in which case you use the next smallest sign that respects the syllable boundary. In the example just cited, you'd use the sign for "there" which is ⠮ because it replaces the most letters out of all of the options.

Example: art ⠜⠞   stand ⠎⠞⠁⠝⠙   still ⠌

Psalm 5:4—For thou ⠜⠞ not a God that hath pleasure in wickedness: neither shall evil dwell with thee.

Psalm 4:4— ⠌⠁⠝⠙ in awe, and sin not: commune with your own he⠜t upon your bed, and be ⠌. Selah.

EXERCISE 12.1

Note: "should," "were," "ound," and "must" have their own contractions, but for now we will use the contraction "sh" for should (⠩), "er" in were (⠻), "ou" in sound (⠳), and "st" in must (⠌).

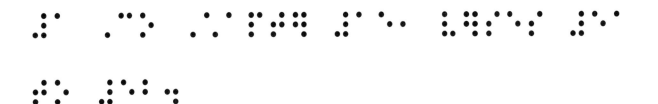

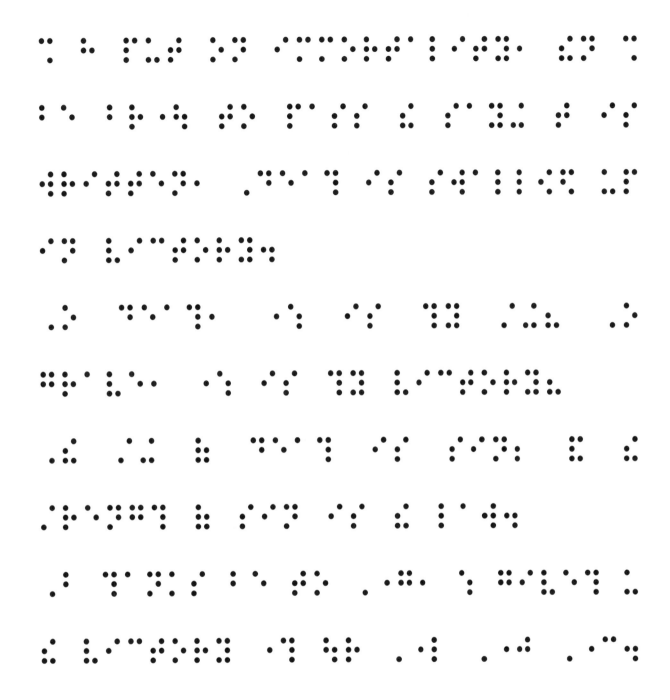

EXERCISE 12.2

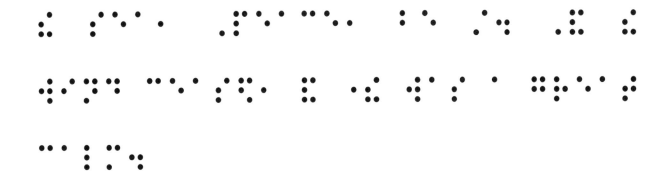

EXERCISE **12.3**

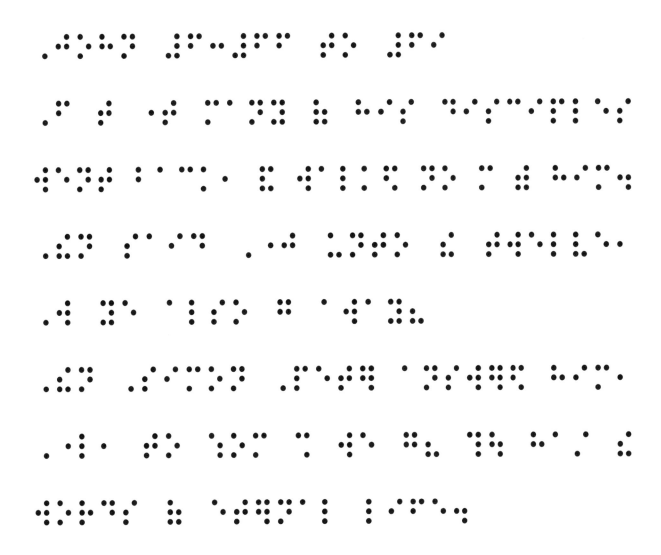

Lesson 13: Wordsigns - Using Dots 4 and 5

Simple	Wordsign		Initial Wordsign		
u	us	⠥	Dots 4, 5 and u	upon	⠨⠥
w	will	⠺	Dots 4, 5 and w	word	⠨⠺
	the	⠮	Dots 4, 5 and the	these	⠨⠮
th	this	⠹	Dots 4, 5 and th	those	⠨⠹
wh	which	⠱	Dots 4, 5 and wh	whose	⠨⠱

The groupsign "word" should be used wherever the letters it represents occur, but "upon," "these," "those," and "whose" must retain their meanings as whole words.

Note: These five can be remembered by the sentence "Upon my word, whose are these and those?"

Examples:

wordy   sword   there   upon

But not:

coupon   theses

In the word "theses" you'd need to use the next best option, which is the "the" sign. Thus, "theses" would be contracted as ⠮⠎⠑⠎ rather than ⠨⠮⠎⠑⠎ .

EXERCISE 13.1

Note: There are Braille contractions for "yourselves," "ourselves," "neither," "would," "should," "such," "their," "ount," "about," "thyself," "together," and "rejoiced," which you haven't learned yet. So for now we will use the Braille signs for "ou" in yourselves, ourselves, would and should; "the" in neither; "ch" in such; "the" in their and together; "ou" in count and about; "th" in thyself; and "ed" in rejoiced.

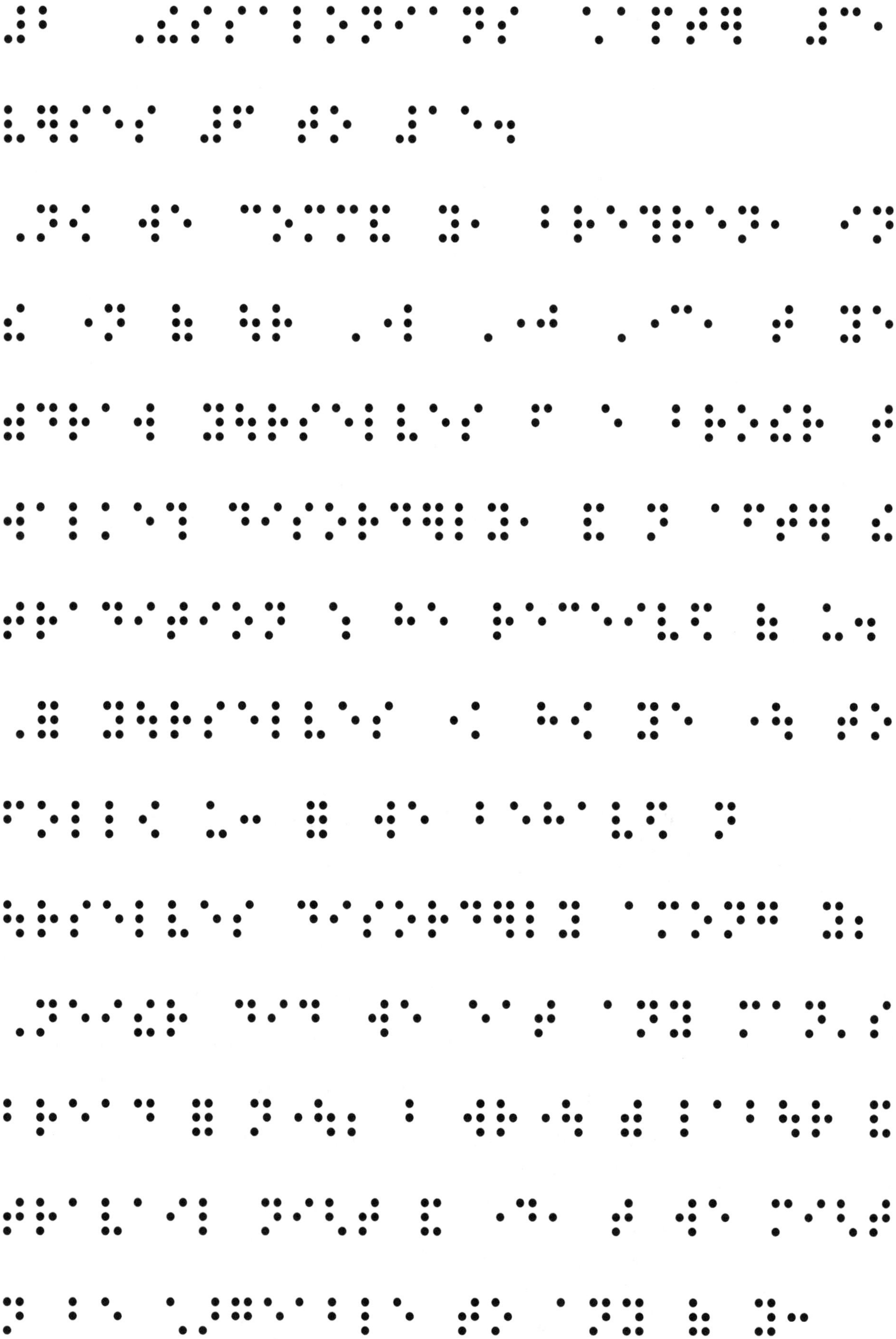

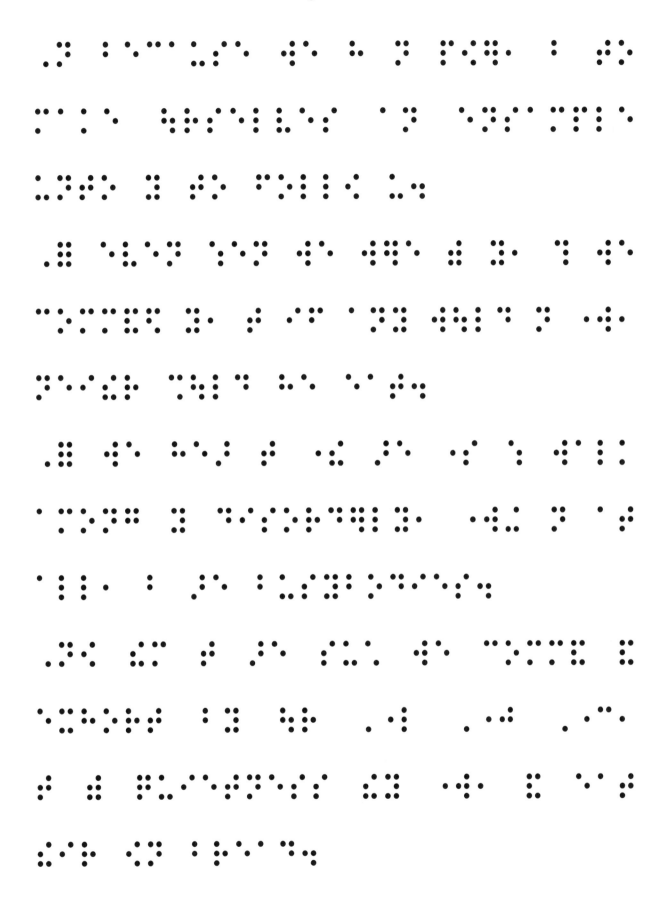

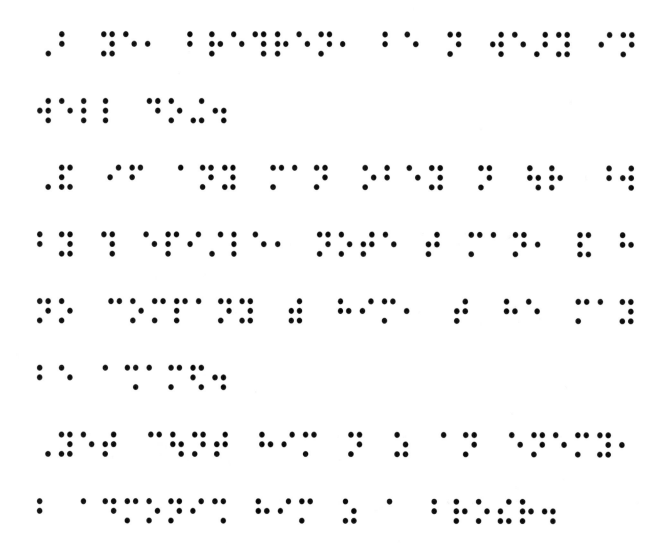

EXERCISE 13.2

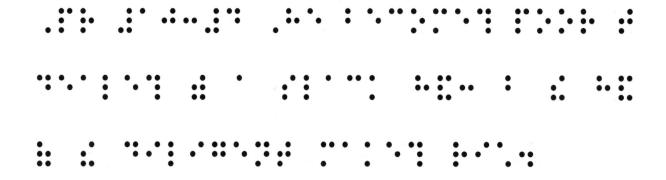

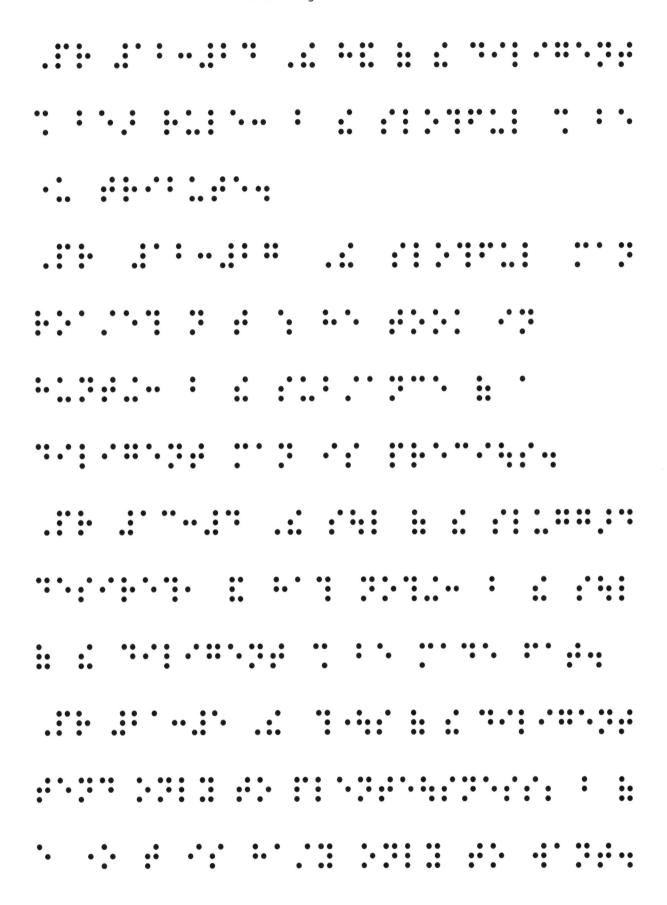

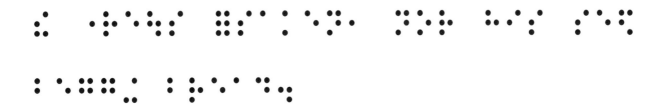

EXERCISE 13.3

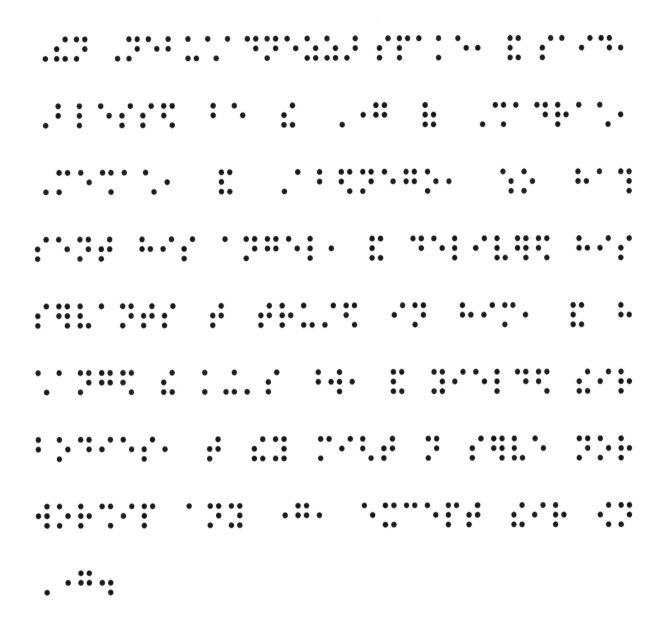

EXERCISE 13.4

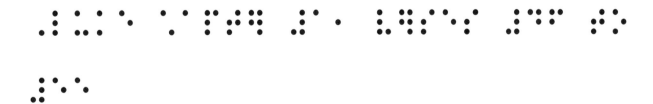

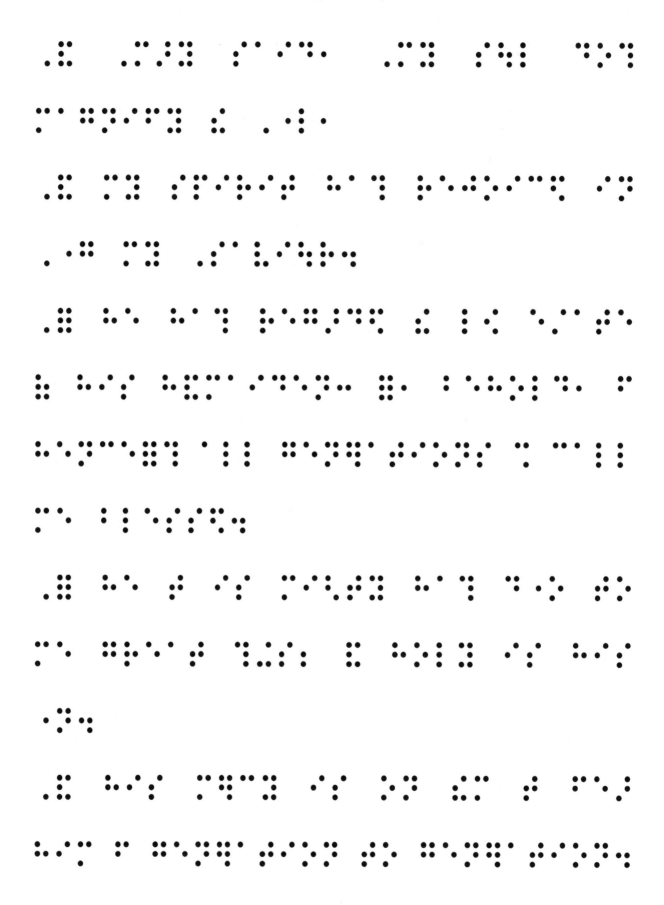

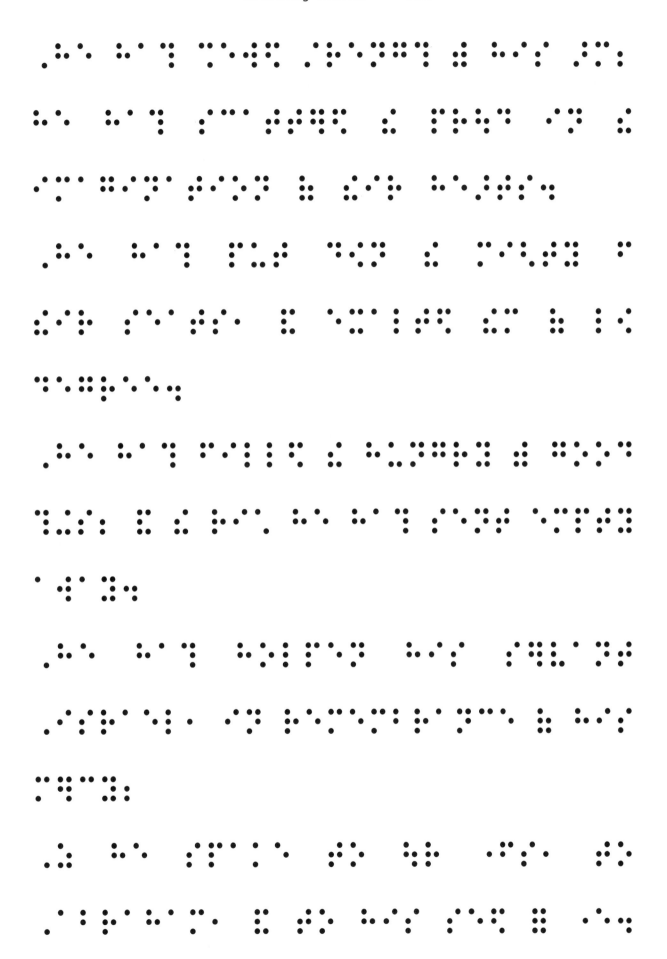

Lesson 14: Initial Wordsigns with Three Dots 4, 5, and 6

Simple	Wordsign		Initial Wordsign		
c	can	⠉	Dots 4, 5, 6 and c	cannot	⠸⠉
h	have	⠓	Dots 4, 5, 6 and h	had	⠸⠓
m	more	⠍	Dots 4, 5, 6 and m	many	⠸⠍
s	so	⠎	Dots 4, 5, 6 and s	spirit	⠸⠎
w	will	⠺	Dots 4, 5, 6 and w	world	⠸⠺
	the	⠮	Dots 4, 5, 6 and the	their	⠸⠮

Apart from "had," these initial wordsigns may generally be used as groupsigns wherever the letters they represent occur. When the "a" is short, "had" may be used as a groupsign.

Example:

hadn't   Germany   spiritual   worldly   theirs

But not:

shade

EXERCISE 14.1

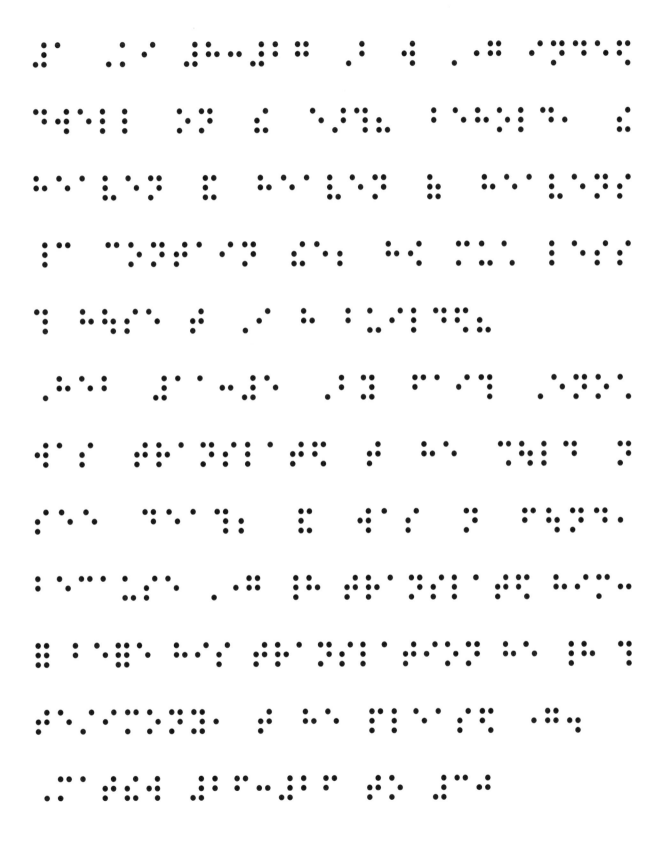

EXERCISE 14.2

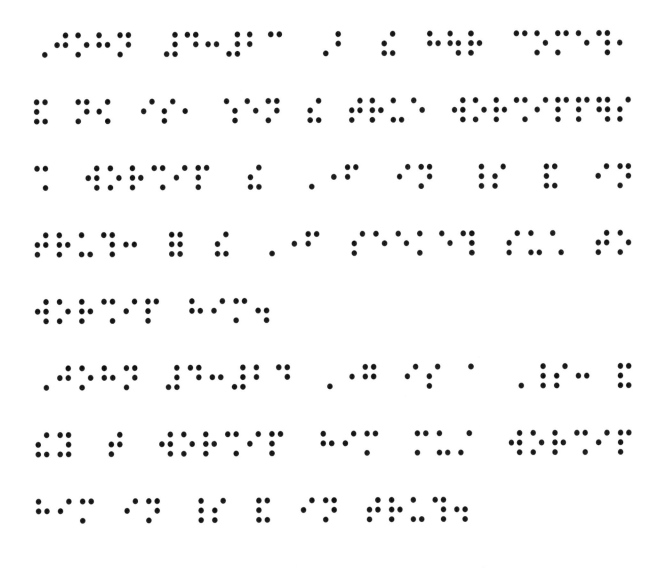

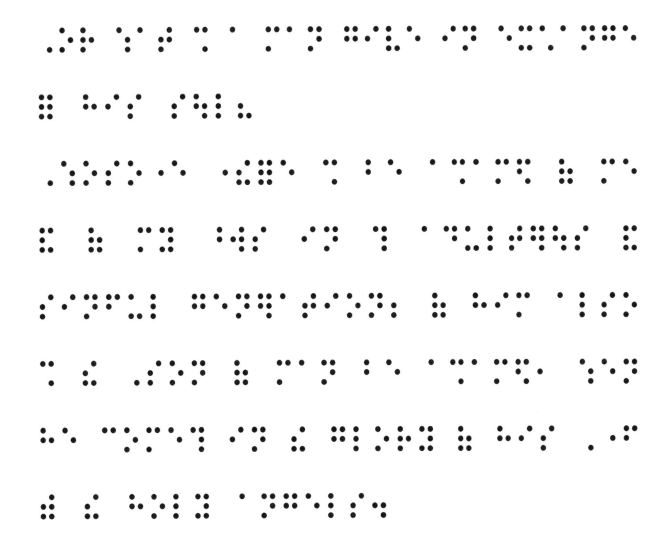

EXERCISE 14.3

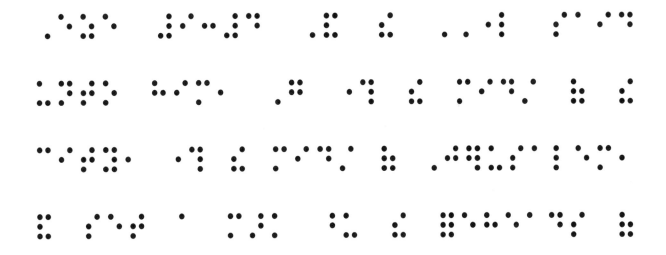

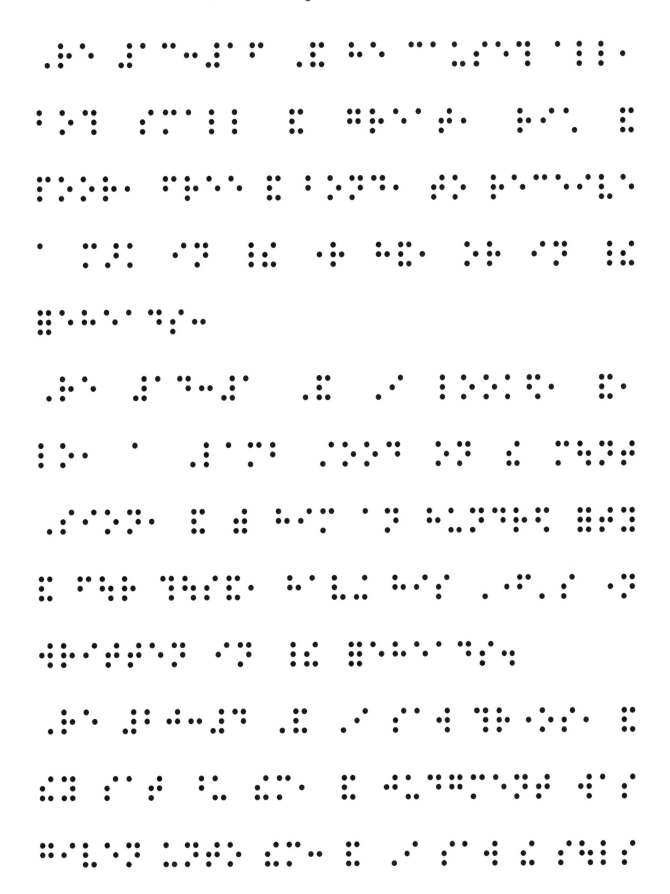

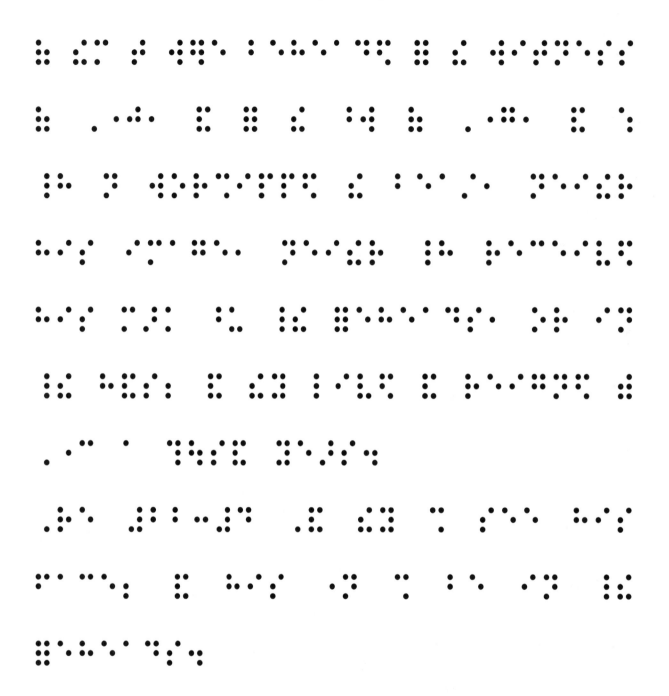

Revision Chart for Wordsigns and Groupsigns

Sign	Simple	Groupsign	Wordsign	Initial Dot 5	Wordsigns Dots 4,5	with Dots 4,5,6
	a		a			
	b		but			
	c		can	Christ		cannot
	d		do	day		
	e		every	ever		
	f		from	father		
	g		go	God		
	h		have	here		had
	i		i			
	j		just	Jesus		
	k		knowledge	know		
	l		like	lord		
	m		more	mother		many
	n		not	name		
	o			one		
	p		people	part		
	q		quite	question		
	r		rather	right		
	s		so	some		spirit
	t		that	time		
	u		us	under	upon	
	v		very			
	w		will	work	word	world
	x		it			
	y		you	young		
	z		as			
		the	the	there	these	their
		ch		character		
		th		through	those	
		wh		where	whose	
		ou		ought		

Lesson 15: Lower Groupsigns

Lower signs are those that have no dots on the top line of the cell. They can be grouped under three headings:

    A.   Those that must be written at the beginning of a word or Braille line.
    B.   Those that must be written in the middle of a word.
    C.   Those that may be written in any part of a word.

Punctuation signs are the only lower signs we have used so far but now the same dots will be used as contractions and wordsigns.

Note: When the stand-alone words "in" and "enough" are adjacent to punctuation, they must not be contracted unless the entire sequence contains a dot in the upper part of the cell. For example, the "in" in the word "father-in-law" may be contracted because "father" and "law" contain dots in the upper part of the cell. But in the sentence "Which draw is the book in?" the "in" must be spelled out.

Lower Groupsigns at the Beginning of a Word or Braille Line

be	con	dis
dots 2, 3	dots 2, 5	dots 2, 5, 6
(lower b)	(middle c)	(lower d)

These three may only be used when they form the first syllable of a word or, in the case of a divided word, the first syllable at the beginning of a Braille line.

Example:

be content

Wrong use of "be":

disobedient should be disobedient

(**Note:** There is a Braille contraction for "en" but you haven't learned it yet.)

Philippians 4:11—Not that I speak in respect of want: for I have learned, in whatsoever state I am, *therewith* to

Titus 1:16—They profess that they know God; but in works they deny *him*, being abominable, and ⠈⠃ ⠙⠊ ⠚⠃ ⠕⠃ ⠊⠉ ⠑⠃ ⠋⠃ ⠛⠃, and unto every good work reprobate.

Exercise 15.1

Note: There are Braille contractions for "about," "bound," "must," "such," "ourselves," "yourselves," and "your," which we haven't learned yet. So for now, we will use the Braille signs for "ou" in ab<u>ou</u>t, b<u>ou</u>nd, <u>ou</u>rselves, y<u>ou</u>rselves, and y<u>ou</u>r; "st" in mu<u>st</u> and "ch" in su<u>ch</u>.

Reminder: The "be," "con," and "dis" contractions can only be used at the beginning of words. The "be" contraction can also only be used when it forms its own syllable. Thus, in words such as "been," "best," "bed," "beast," "bearing," etc., you cannot use it.

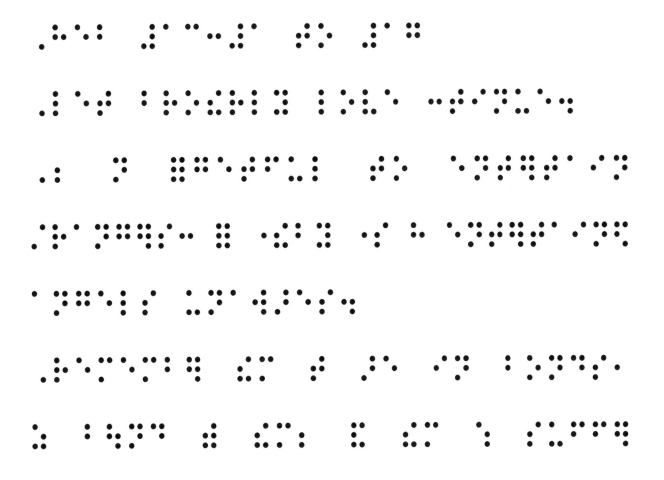

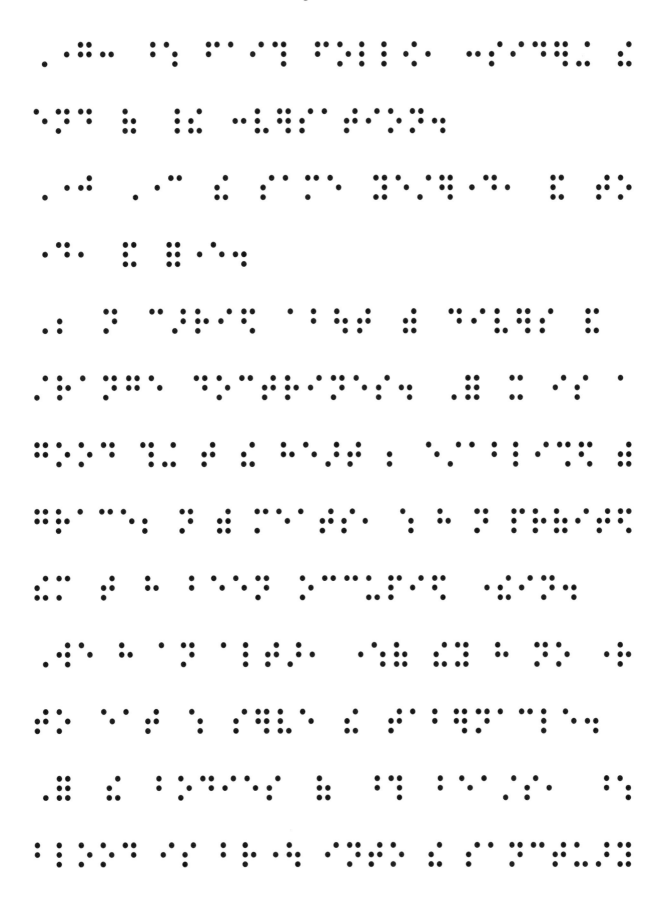

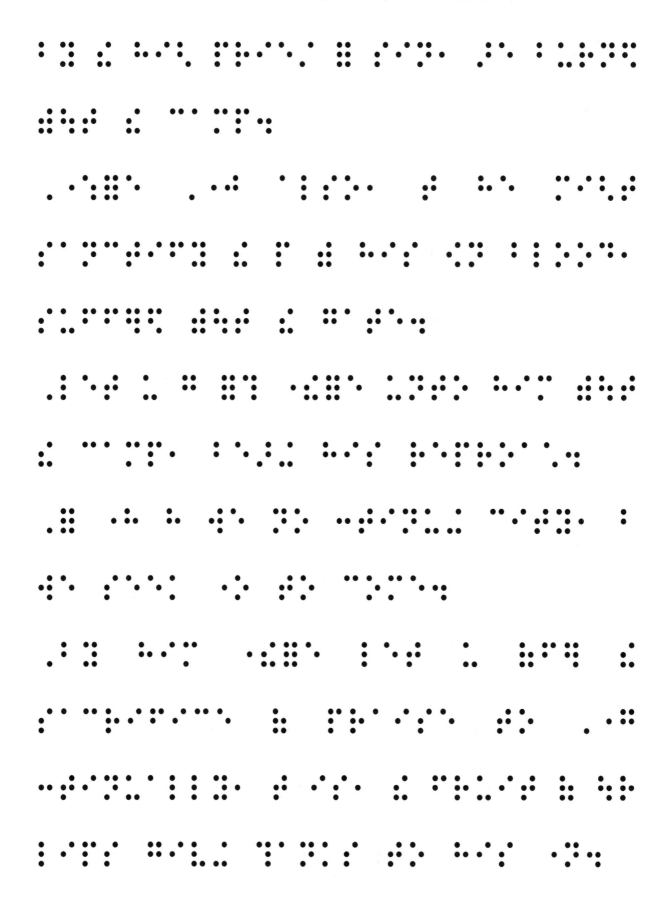

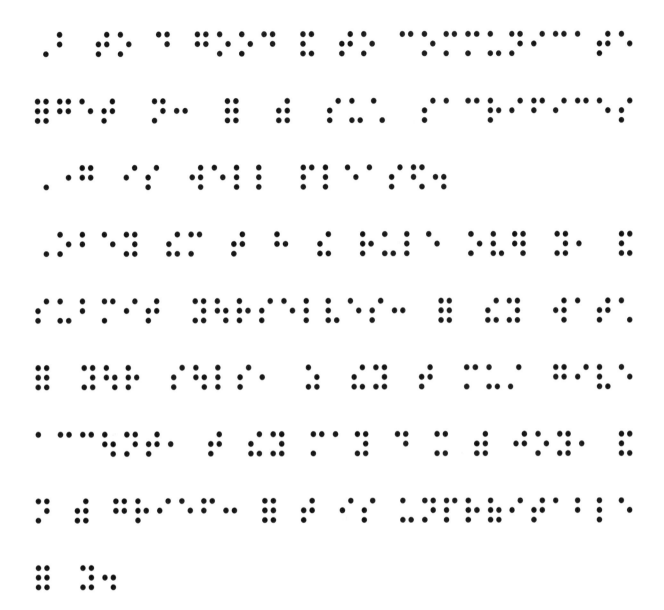

EXERCISE 15.2

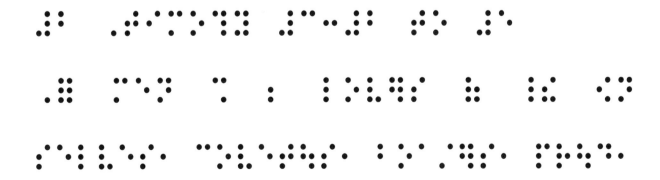

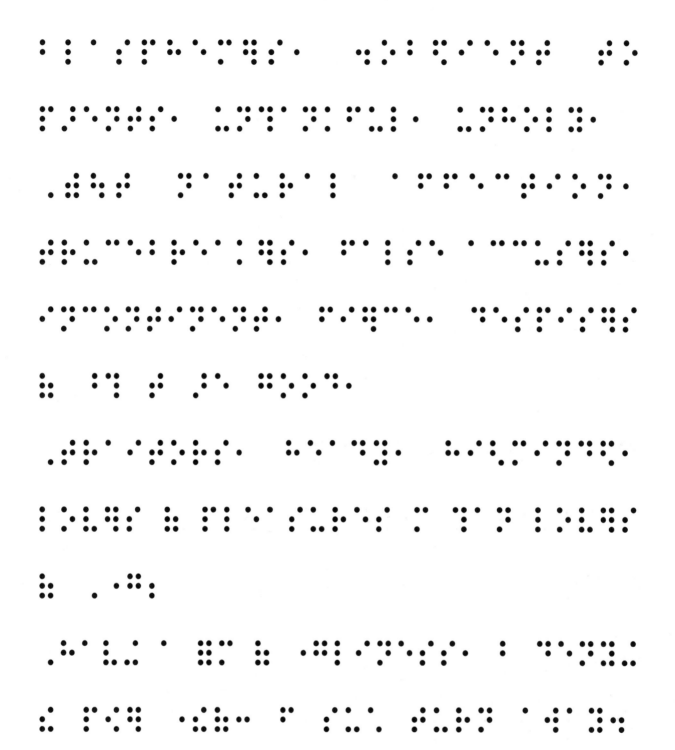

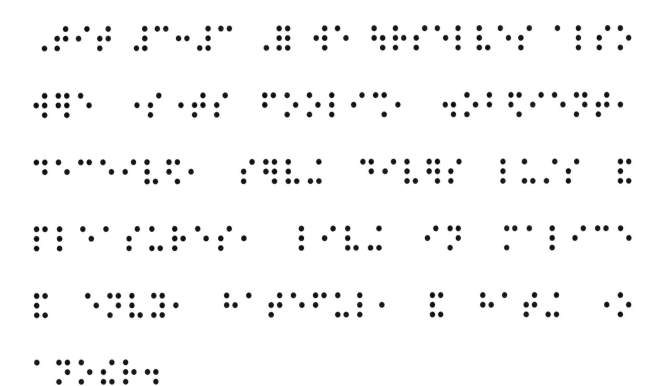

Lesson 16: Hyphen and Dash

The Hyphen (-) ⠤ dots 3 and 6 (bottom c) is used as in print.

The dash (—) ⠠⠤ dots 6, 3 and 6 is written unspaced from the words that precede and follow it, unlike in print where it may be spaced. Also note that the dash must never be split between two lines in Braille.

Example:

The Lord Jesus speaks of child ⠤ like faith ⠠⠤ Luke 18:17 Verily I say unto you, Whosoever shall not receive the kingdom of God as a little child shall in no wise enter therein.

When a word must be hyphenated at a line break, the syllable at the end of the line may end in one of these contractions, and the rest of the word at the start of the following line may also begin with a contraction (as in the example above). Even the contraction for "ing" may begin a new line to complete a hyphenated word.

There are two types of compound words.

(a) Hyphenated: as in "child-like"
(b) Unhyphenated: as in "aircraft"

When a word is hyphenated in the printed text, each hyphenated word is considered distinct and may be brailled using the appropriate wordsign.

Example: child-like ⠡⠇⠙⠤⠇⠅

Where the word is not hyphenated in the print and thus the word is considered a single word, wordsigns may not be used.

Example: childlike ⠡⠊⠇⠙⠇⠊⠅⠑

Exercise 16.1

There is only one instance of the use of a dash in the Holy Bible. Please transcribe the following.

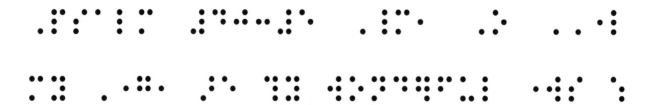

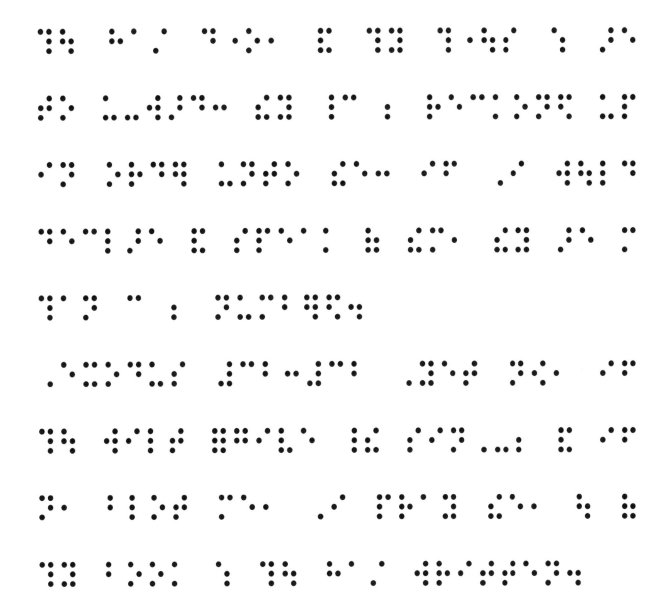

Lesson 17: Lower Groupsigns in the Middle of a Word

<u>ea</u>	<u>bb</u>	<u>cc</u>	<u>ff</u>	<u>gg</u>
dot 2	dots 2,3	dots 2, 5	dots 2,3, 5	dots 2,3,5, 6
(middle a)	(middle b)	(middle c)	(middle f)	(middle g)
⠂	⠆	⠒	⠲	⠶

Examples:

h<u>ea</u>vens

ro<u>bb</u>ery

a<u>cc</u>ord

Note: All of the contractions in the above table may only be used in the middle of a word. You cannot, for example, use the "ea" contraction in the word "earth," or the "ff" contraction in the word "stuff."

"Himself," "themselves," "found," "should," "were," "children," and "such" have their own Braille contractions but you have not learned those yet so for now we will just use the contractions you have learned.

EXERCISE 17.1

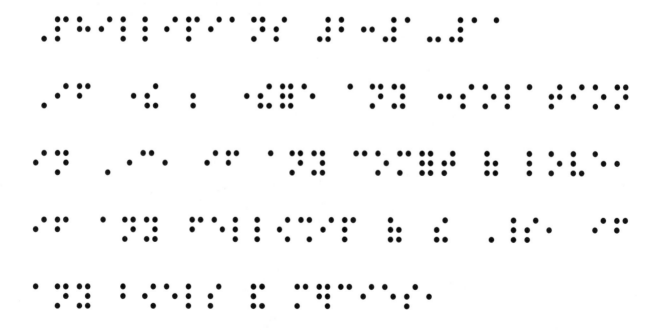

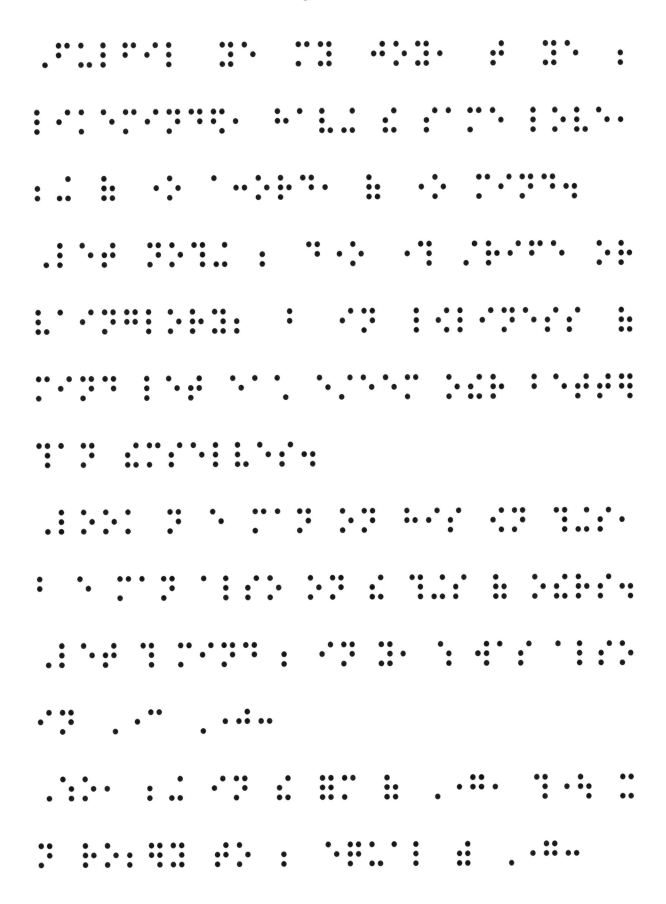

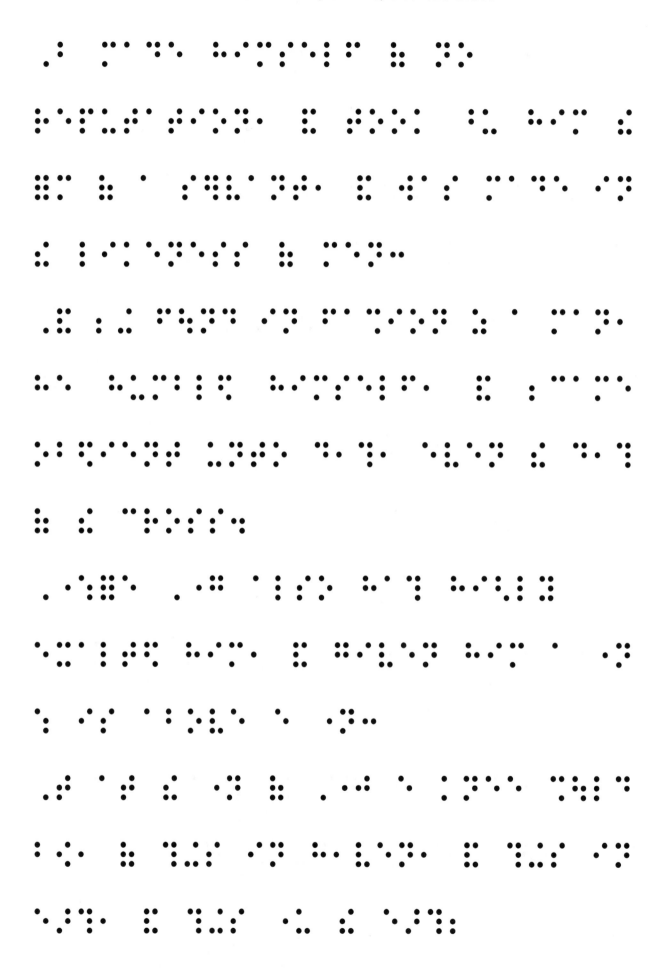

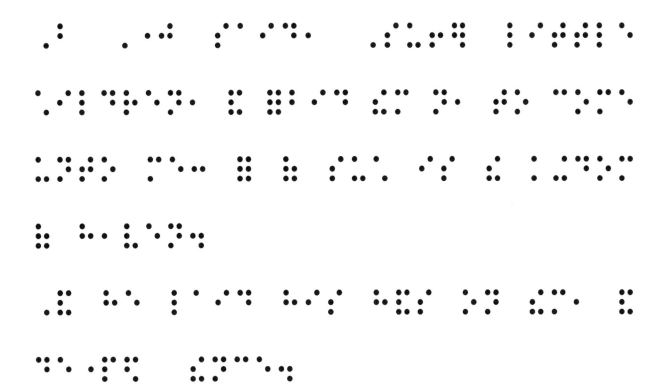

Lesson 18: Round Brackets or Parentheses

Open Bracket/Parentheses	Closed Bracket/Parentheses
⠦	⠴

Example:

1 Timo<u>th</u>y 3:5 (<u>For</u> if a man <u>know</u> <u>not</u> <u>how</u> to rule his <u>own</u> house, <u>how</u> <u>shall</u> he take ca<u>re</u> <u>of</u> <u>the</u> <u>ch</u>ur<u>ch</u> <u>of</u> <u>God</u>?)

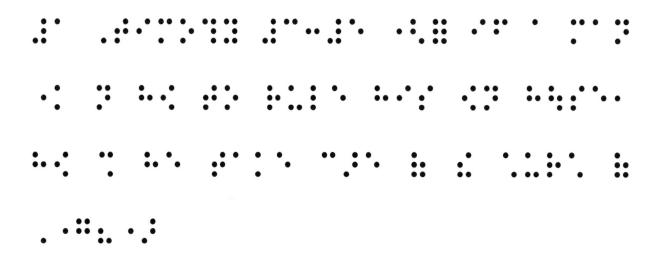

Exercise 18.1

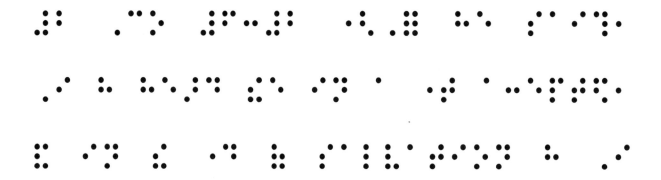

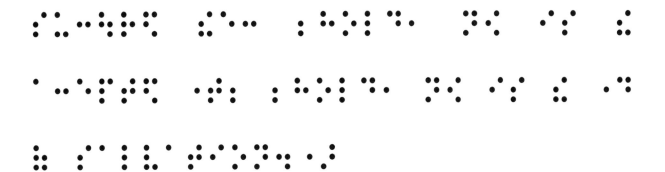

Lesson 19: Lower Groupsigns in Any Part of a Word

en	in
dots 2, 6 (lower e)	dots 3, 5 (lower i)
⠢	⠔

These two lower groupsigns may be used in any part of a word. They are the only lower groupsigns that may be used at the end of a word.

Example:

broken ⠃⠗⠕⠅⠢

length ⠇⠑⠝⠛⠹

curtain ⠉⠥⠗⠞⠔

beginning ⠃⠑⠛⠔⠝⠬

EXERCISE 19.1

Note: Remember that when the stand-alone words "in" and "enough" are adjacent to punctuation, they must not be contracted unless the entire sequence contains a dot in the upper part of the cell. For example, the "in" in the word "father-in-law" may be contracted because "father" and "law" contain dots in the upper part of the cell. In the following exercise, the "in" followed by the colon cannot be contracted because there is no dot in the upper part of the cell in the entire sequence.

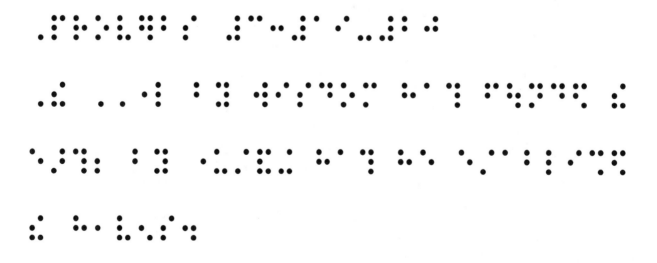

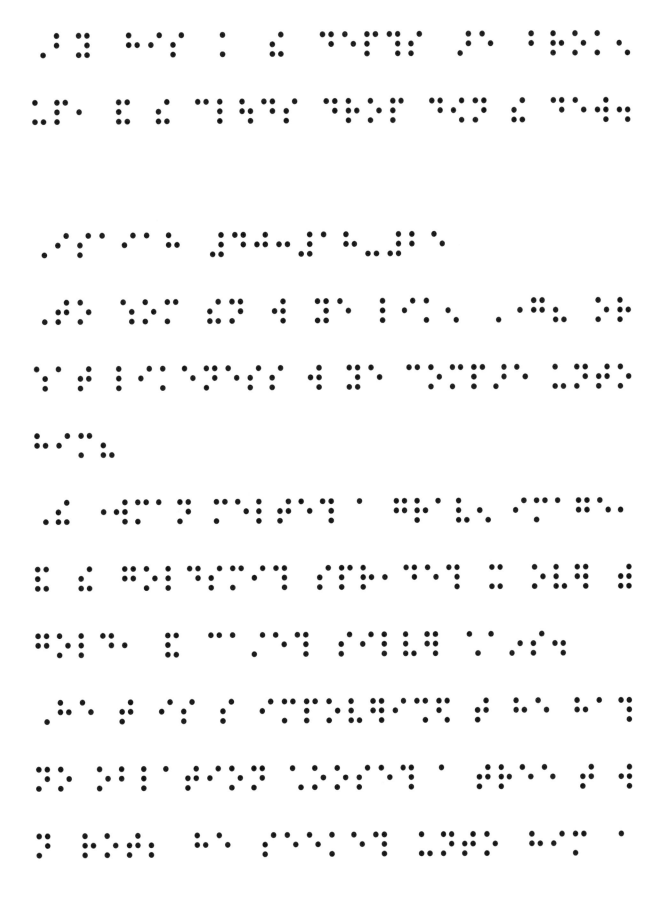

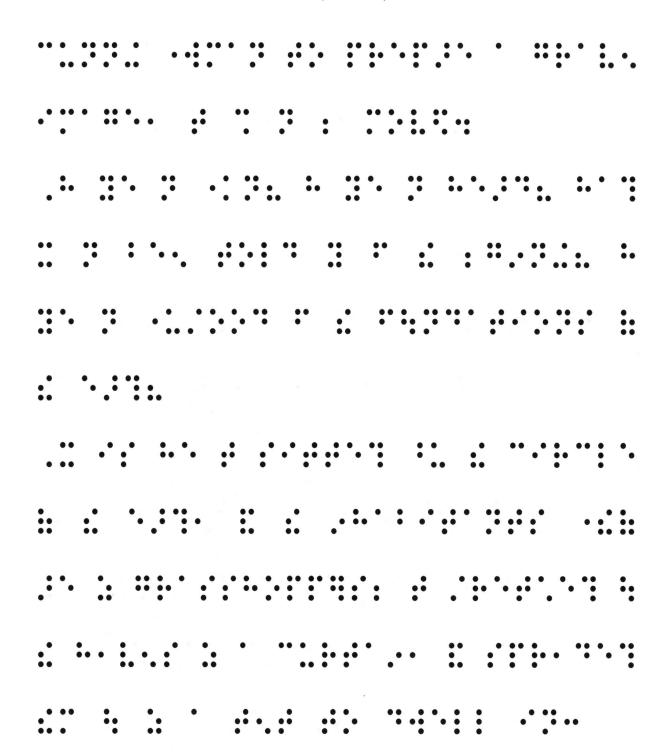

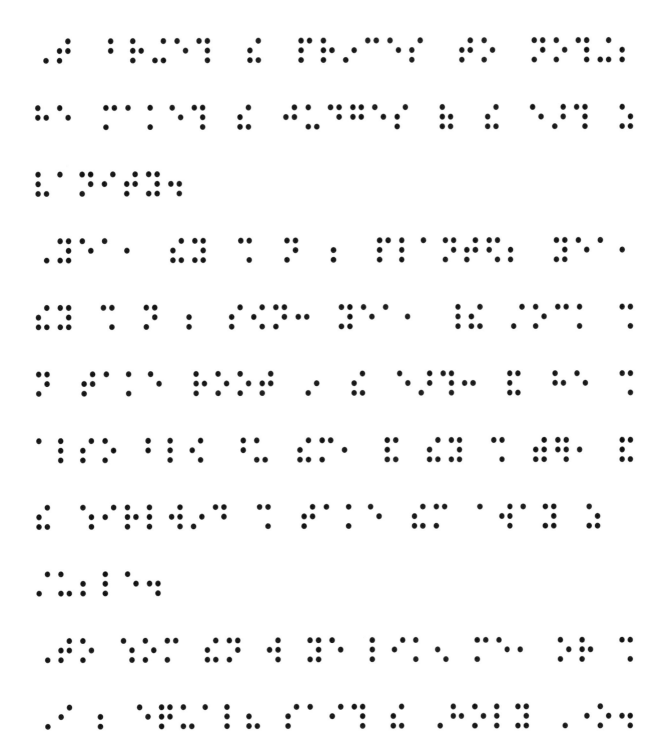

Lesson 20: Lower Wordsigns

Some of the lower signs are also used as wordsigns to represent whole words. They can be grouped under two headings:

1. Those that must be spaced from all other signs.
2. Those that must be spaced from all other words but may in some cases be in contact with punctuation signs.

Lower wordsigns that must be spaced from all other signs:

be	were	his	was
dots 2, 3	dots 2, 3, 5, 6	dots 2, 3, 6	dots 3, 5, 6
(lower b)	(lower g)	(lower h)	(lower j)

Lower wordsigns that must be spaced from all other words but may in some cases be in contact with punctuation signs:

enough	in
dots 2, 6 (lower e)	dots 3,5

When used as wordsigns these two signs must be spaced from all other words, but they may be used adjoining punctuation signs if the whole sequence is in contact with an upper sign.

Example:

enough's enough!

The first "enough" is followed immediately by punctuation """ but the whole sequence is adjoining an "s," which has a dot in the upper part of the cell. The second "enough" is also followed by punctuation but since the whole sequence is not joined to a symbol with dots in the upper part of the cell, the wordsign can't be used. Instead, we must use the "en" symbol followed by the "ou" symbol, followed by the "gh" symbol. The rationale of disallowing lower wordsigns from being used if joined to other lower wordsigns that are not adjoining a symbol with dots in the upper cell is to avoid confusion—the reader will not be able to distinguish whether the whole sequence is in the upper or lower part of the cell without dots in the upper part of the cell to give a point of reference.

EXERCISE **20.1**

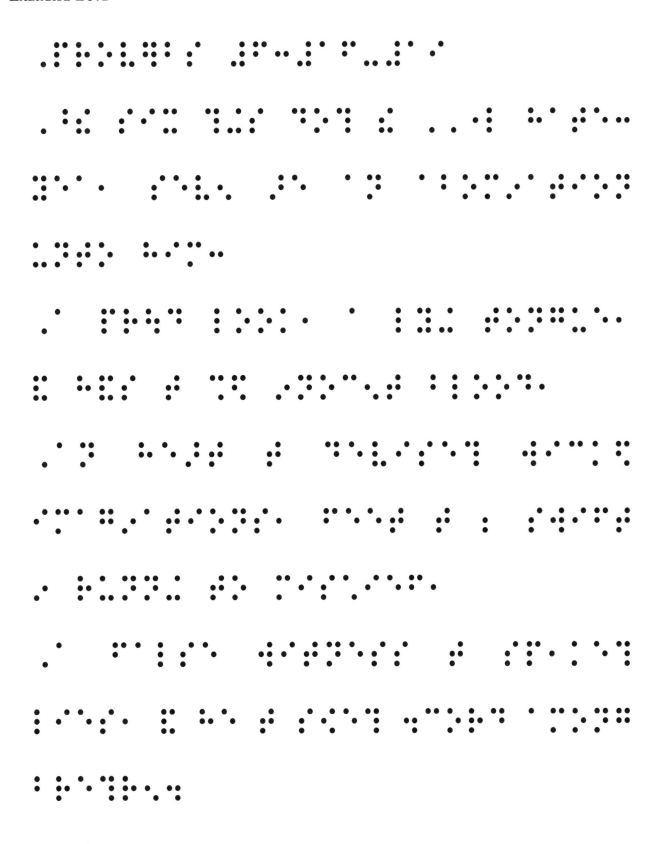

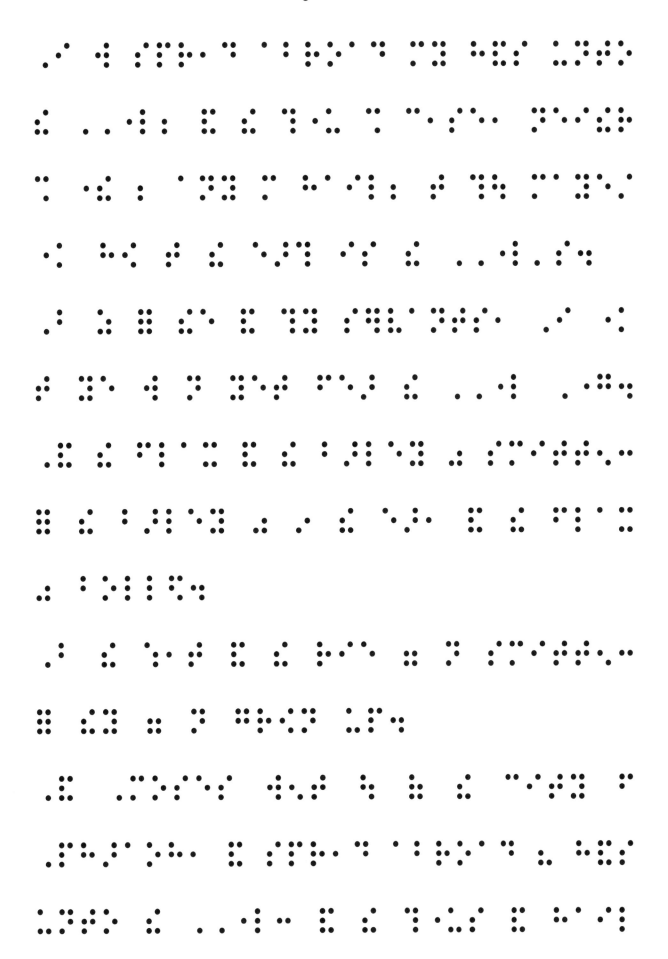

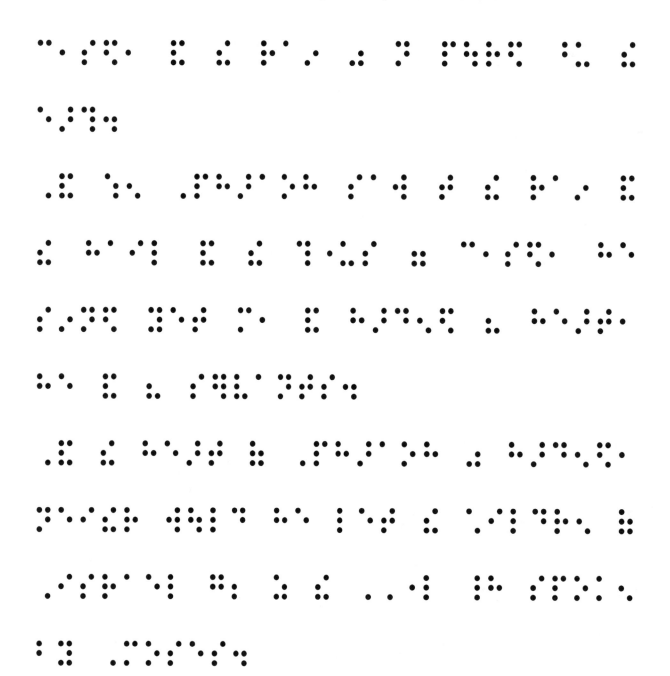

Lesson 21: Groupsigns

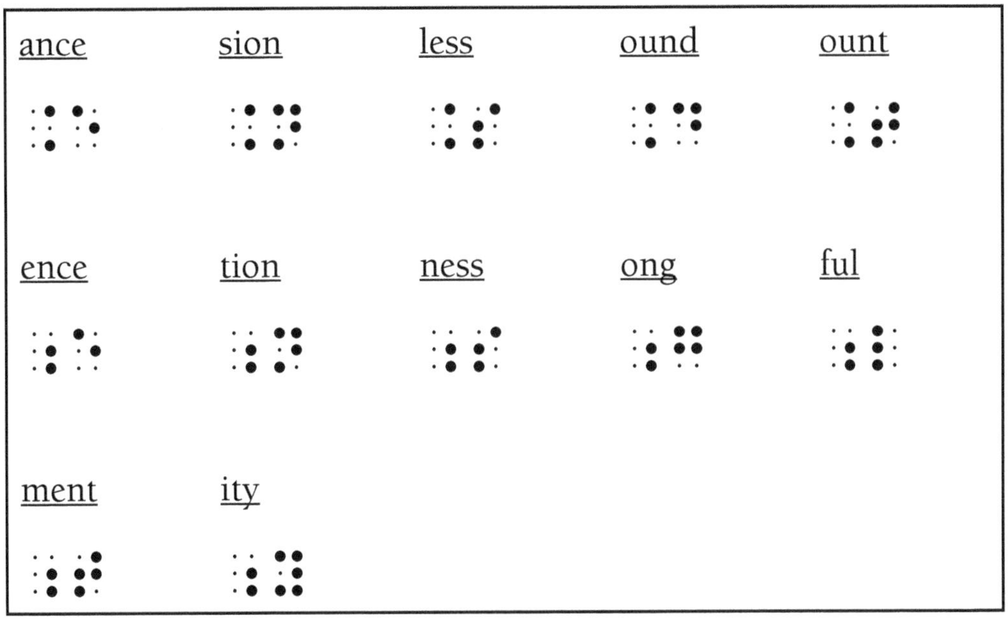
ance
sion
less
ound
ount
ence
tion
ness
ong
ful
ment
ity

Examples:

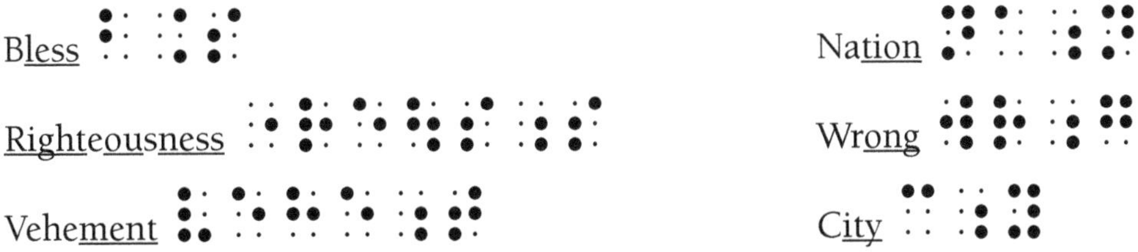
Bless
Righteousness
Vehement
Nation
Wrong
City

Exercise 21.1

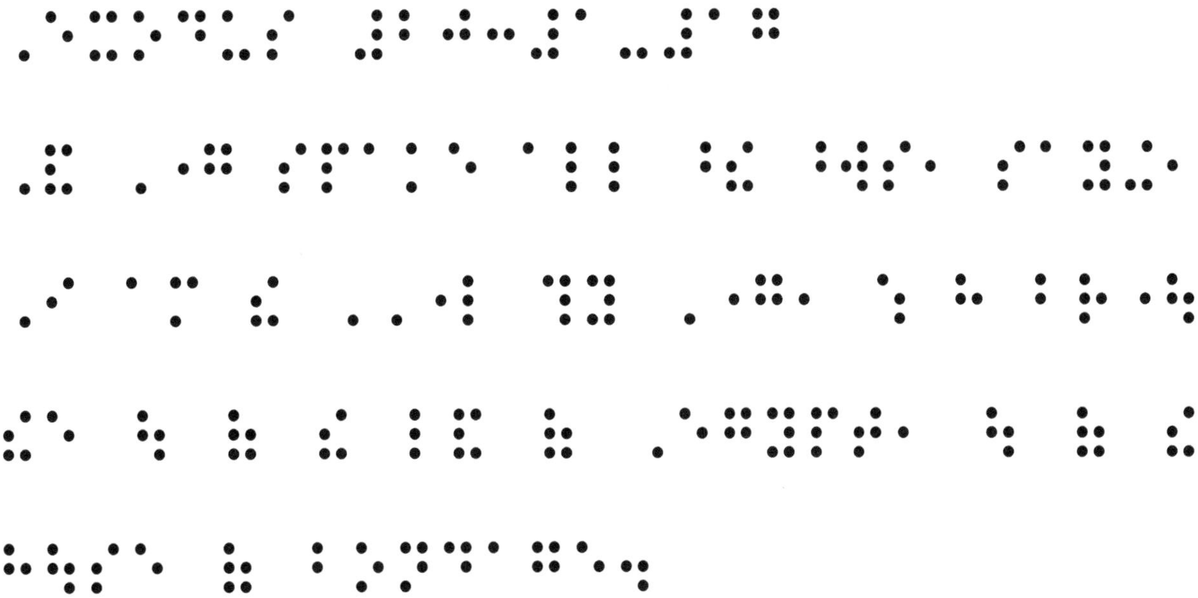

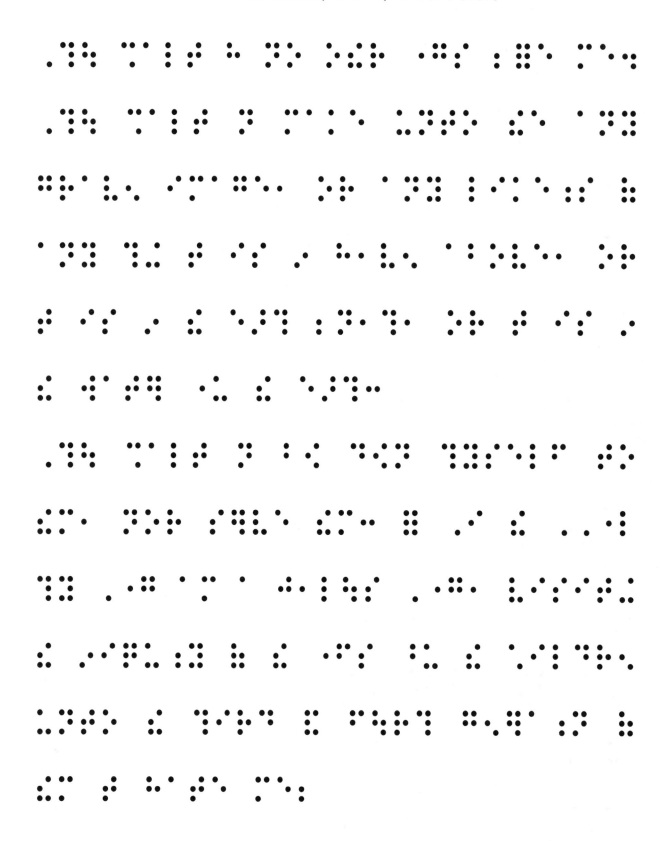

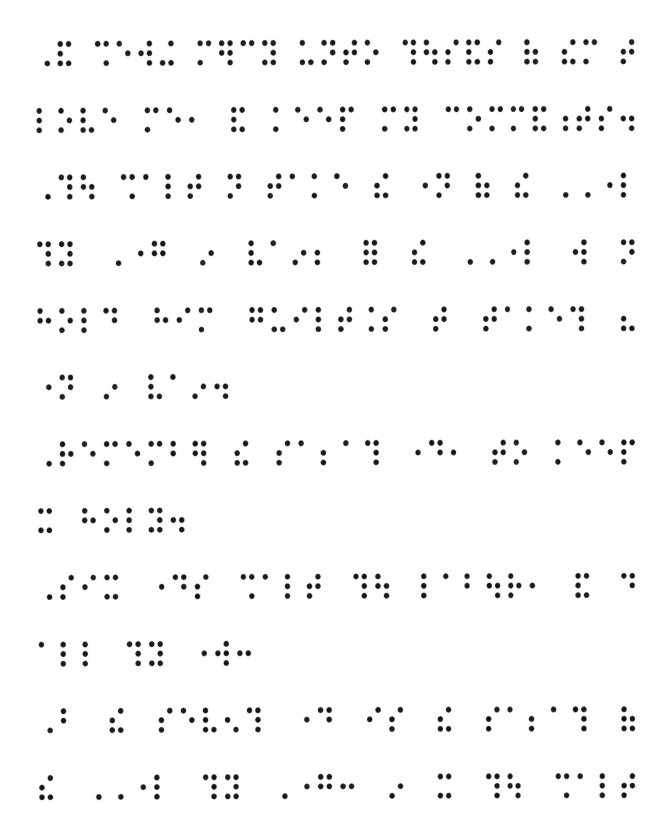

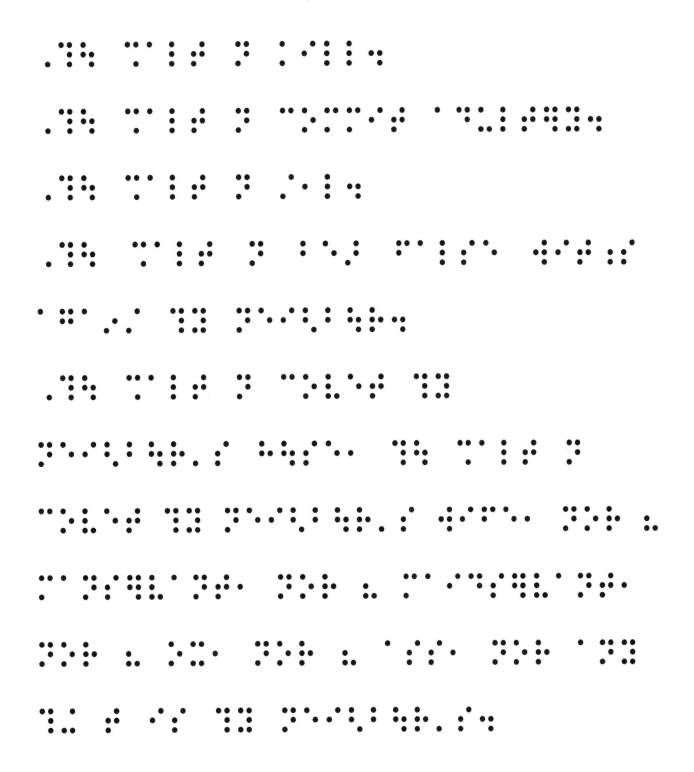

EXERCISE 21.2

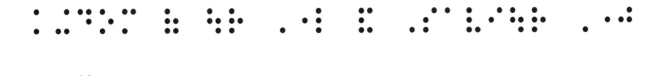

EXERCISE 21.3

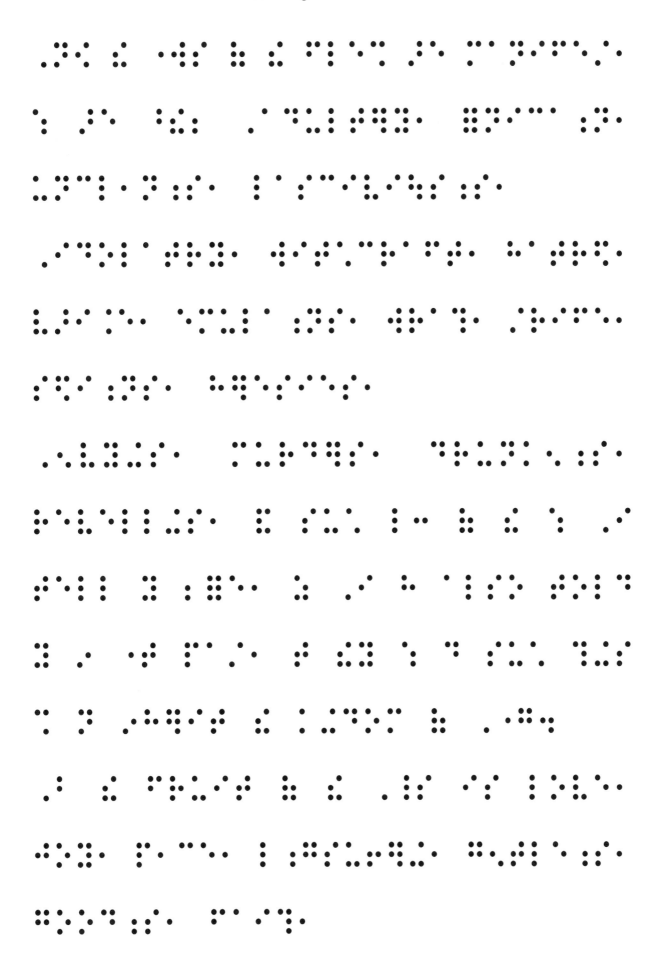

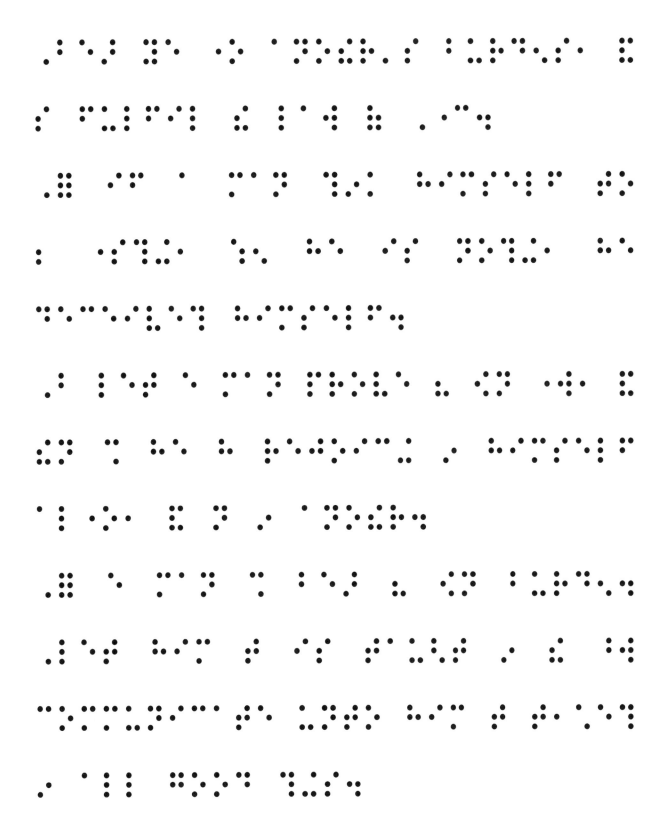

EXERCISE 21.4

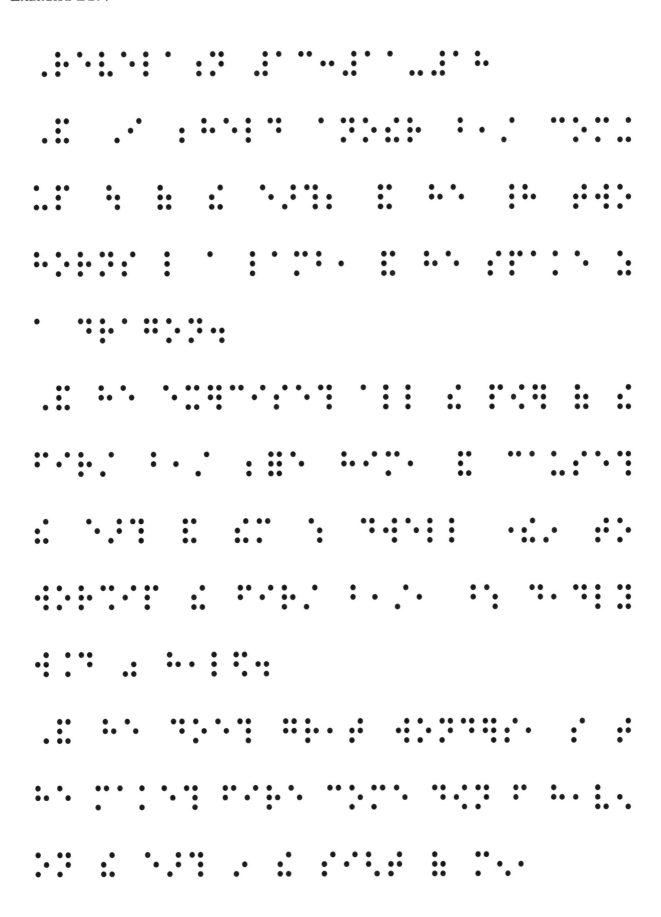

⠐⠃ ⠘⠉⠿⠻⠝⠞ ⠰⠃ ⠌ ⠐⠙⠕⠇ ⠫⠃ ⠒⠊
⠝⠙⠄⠃⠱ ⠰⠃ ⠊⠝⠓ ⠿ ⠝ ⠊⠙⠟⠝⠝⠄ ⠠
⠂⠁ ⠆⠆ ⠐⠿⠹ ⠃⠱ ⠝ ⠄ ⠊⠝⠿ ⠫⠃ ⠰⠃
⠊⠂⠒ ⠒⠿⠹⠱ ⠕⠙ ⠫⠃ ⠌ ⠐⠙⠕⠇ ⠫⠃ ⠒⠊
⠝⠙⠄ ⠌ ⠠⠱ ⠐⠙⠃⠝ ⠒⠹⠝ ⠒⠹ ⠼⠒⠺⠊⠄
⠫⠃ ⠊ ⠆ ⠠ ⠒ ⠊⠃ ⠼⠉⠙⠝⠙⠃⠂ ⠒⠙⠽
⠃⠒ ⠘⠿⠓ ⠒⠱⠺⠺⠓

⠐⠃ ⠆⠃ ⠊⠞ ⠐⠙⠕⠇ ⠫⠃ ⠐⠿⠙⠃⠄ ⠊⠿⠹ ⠰⠄⠓
⠃⠒⠝⠙ ⠫⠃⠇ ⠝ ⠠⠙⠄ ⠌ ⠒⠝⠙ ⠁⠒⠝⠓ ⠫⠃
⠊⠂⠄ ⠐⠹⠝⠙ ⠒⠙⠝ ⠒⠝⠒⠄ ⠿ ⠿⠿⠙ ⠰
⠿ ⠊⠝ ⠰ ⠐⠹⠝⠙ ⠘ ⠐⠿⠙⠒⠝ ⠫ ⠒⠙⠺
⠿ ⠃⠝⠄⠽ ⠐⠹⠝⠙ ⠘ ⠰ ⠊⠒⠝⠞⠺

Lesson 22: Shortforms

The underlined letters "st, th, be, ch" in the following chart show which group signs to use in these contractions. For example, in the shortform "bec for because", the "be" groupsign is used with the letter "c" like this ⠿⠿⠿

The letter sign, dots 56 must be used before a letter or group of letters which could otherwise be misinterpreted as a word. For example, the book abbreviation for Acts is Ac. Because the letters Ac would be interpreted as the word According, we must preceed it with the letter sign. Another example is if we wish to write the letter b. Usually a b by itself would be read as "but." So that the reader knows we mean b, it must be preceded by dots 56. The letter sign is written immediately prior to the letter or letters, without an intervening space.

about	ab	conceive	concv	ourselves	ourvs
above	abv	conceiving	concvg	paid	pd
according	ac	could	cd	perceive	percv
across	acr	deceive	dcv	perceiving	percvg
after	af	deceiving	dcvg	perhaps	perh
afternoon	afn	declare	dcl	quick	qk
afterward	afw	declaring	dclg	receive	rcv
again	ag	either	ei	receiving	rcvg
against	agst	first	fst	rejoice	rjc
almost	alm	friend	fr	rejoicing	rjcg
already	alr	good	gd	said	sd
also	al	great	grt	should	shd
although	alth	herself	herf	such	sch
altogether	alt	him	hm	themselves	themvs
always	alw	himself	hmf	thyself	thyf
because	bec	immediate	imm	today	td
before	bef	its	xs	together	tg
behind	beh	itself	xf	tomorrow	tm
below	bel	letter	lr	tonight	tn
beneath	ben	little	ll	would	wd
beside	bes	much	mch	your	yb
between	bet	must	mst	yourself	yrf

beyond	bey	myself	myf	yourselves	yrvs
blind	bl	necessary	nec		
Braille	Brl	neither	nei		
children	chn	oneself	onef		

EXERCISE 22.1 A

There are no verses in the King James Bible containing the words "across," "Braille," "oneself," "today," "tomorrow," "tonight," "yourself" or "yourselves." Note: The King James Version spells "today" as two words ("to day") and "tomorrow" as "to morrow," which are still contracted as td and tm respectively.

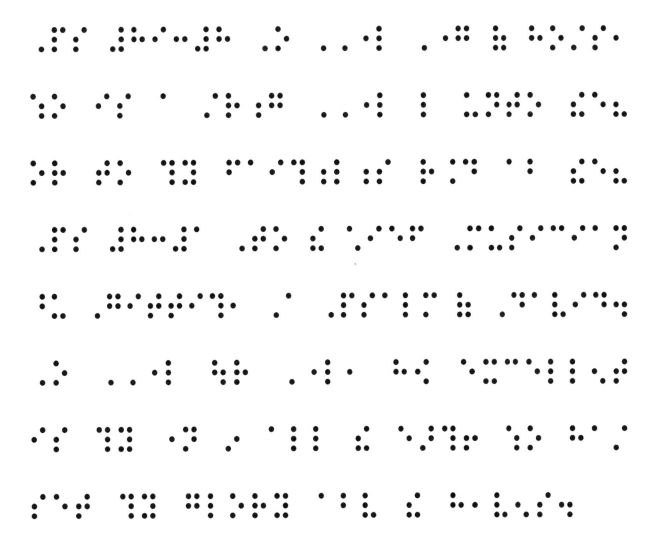

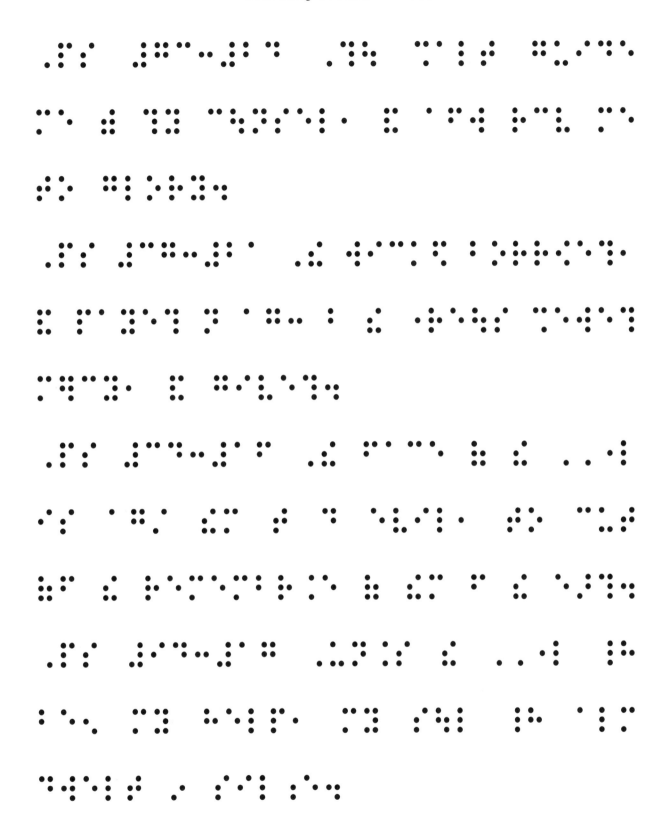

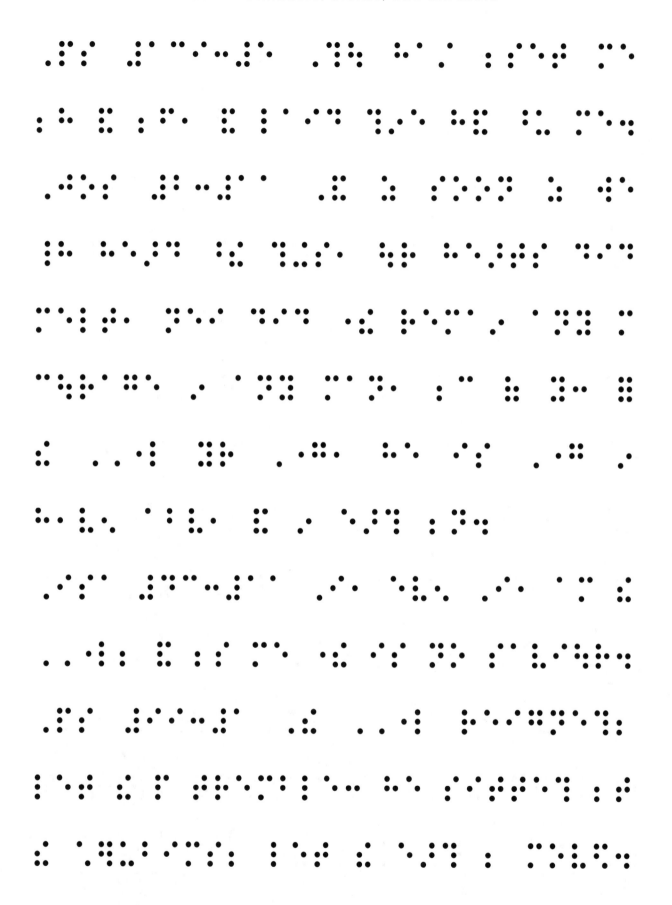

Exercise 22.1 B

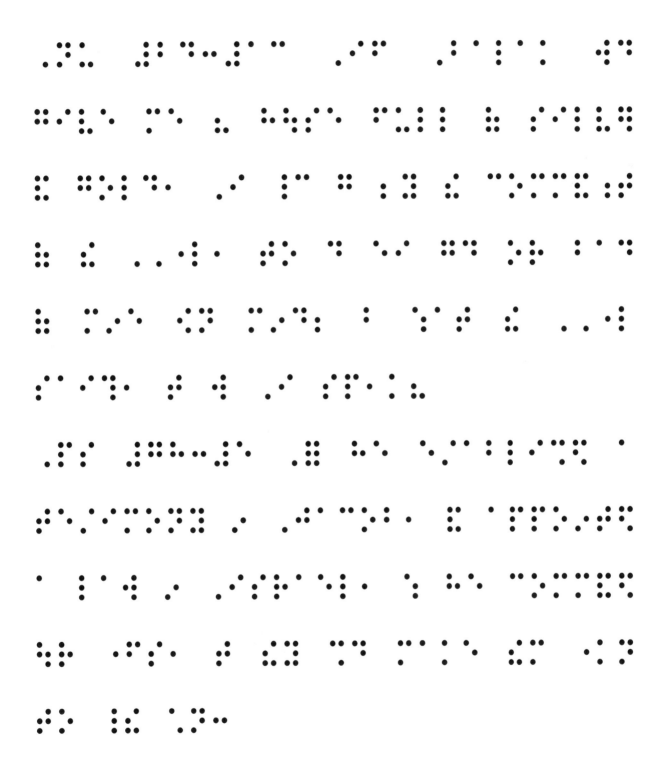

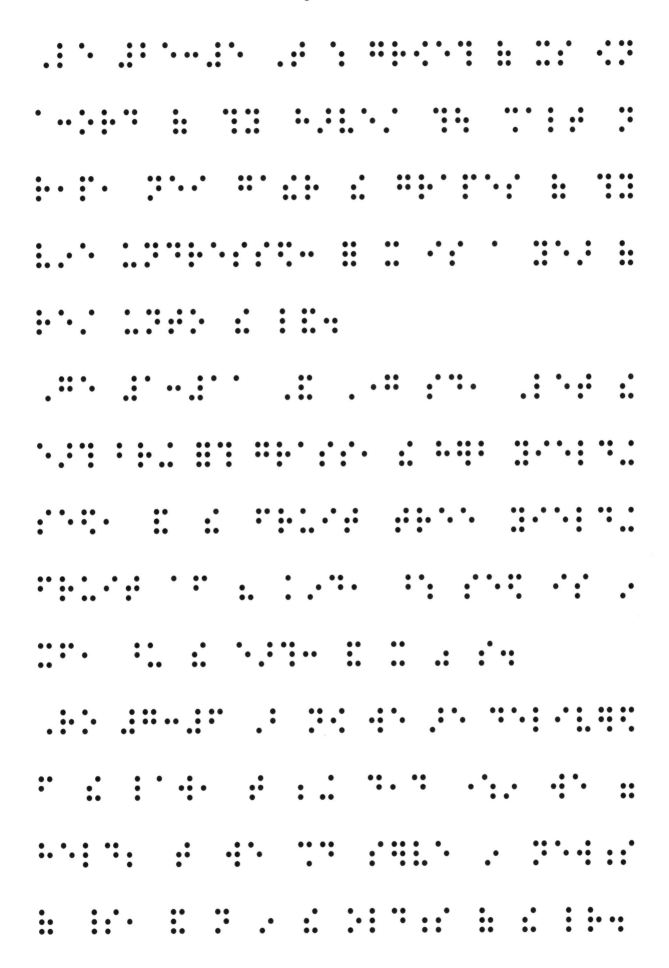

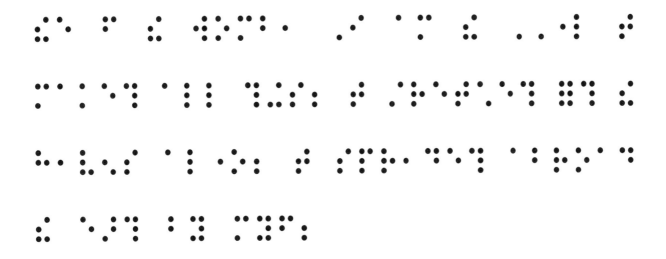

EXERCISE 22.1 C

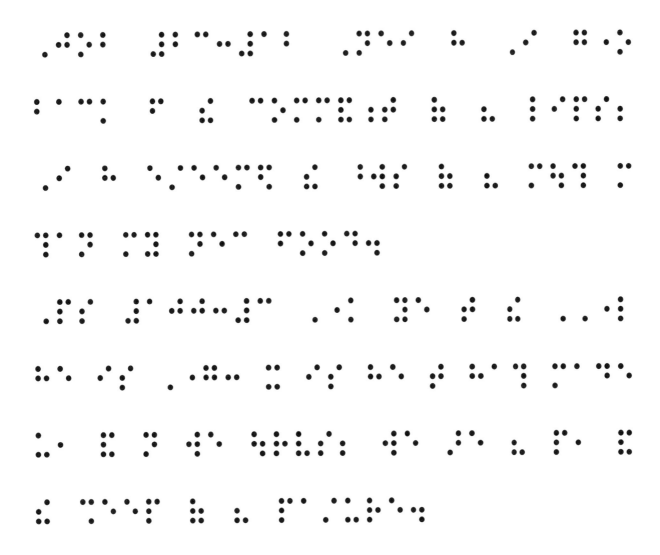

EXERCISE 22.2 A

Below are all the verses found in the Holy Bible to do with the blind.

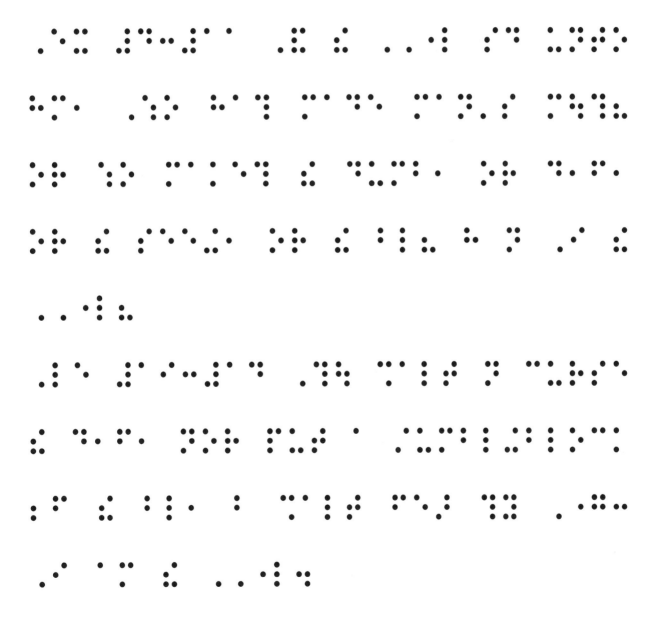

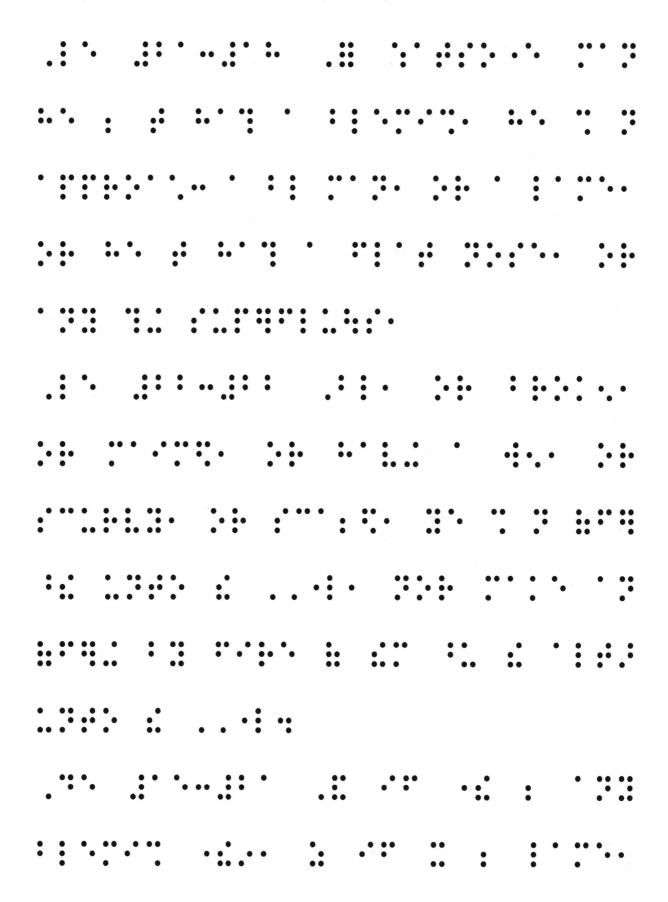

EXERCISE 22.2 B

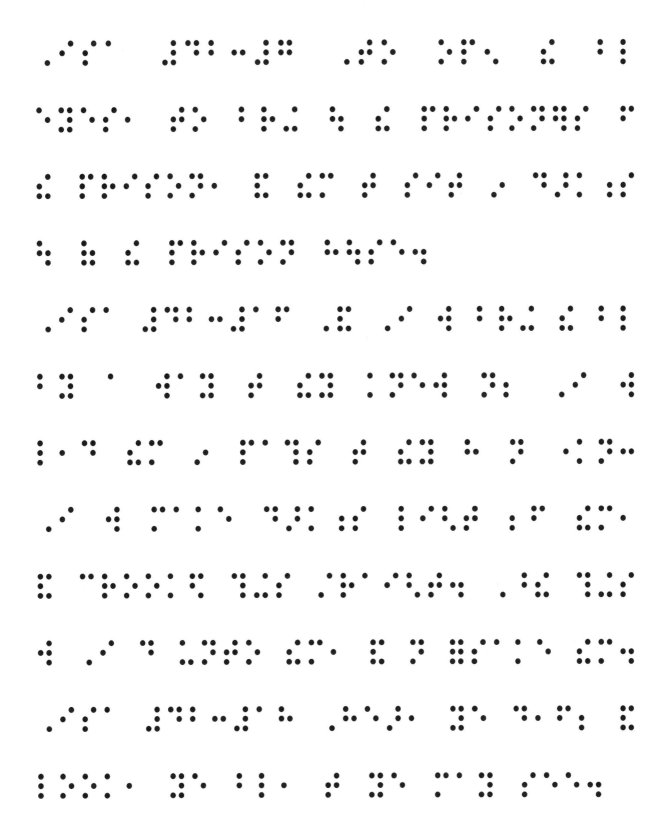

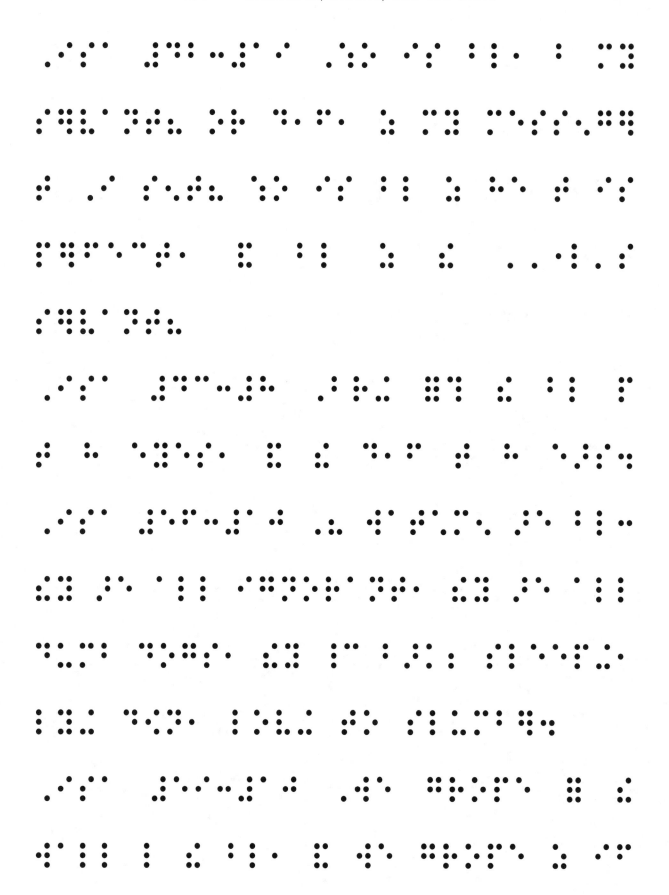

EXERCISE 22.2 C

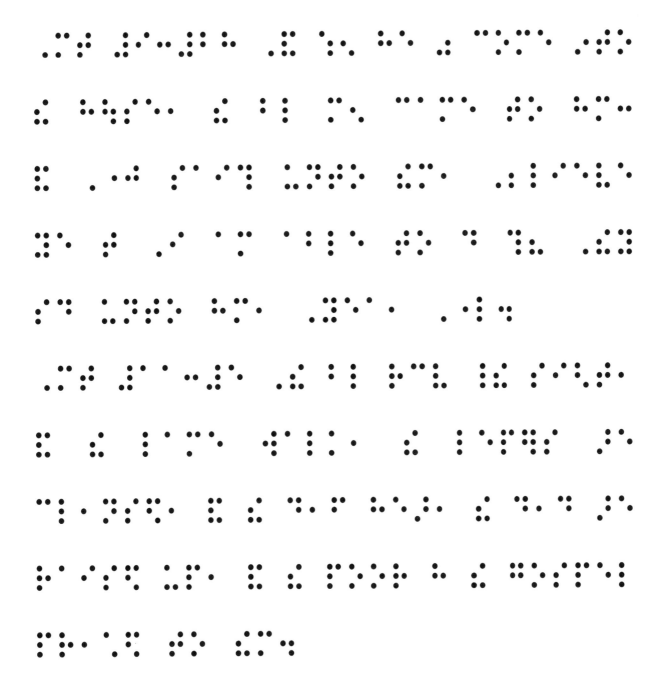

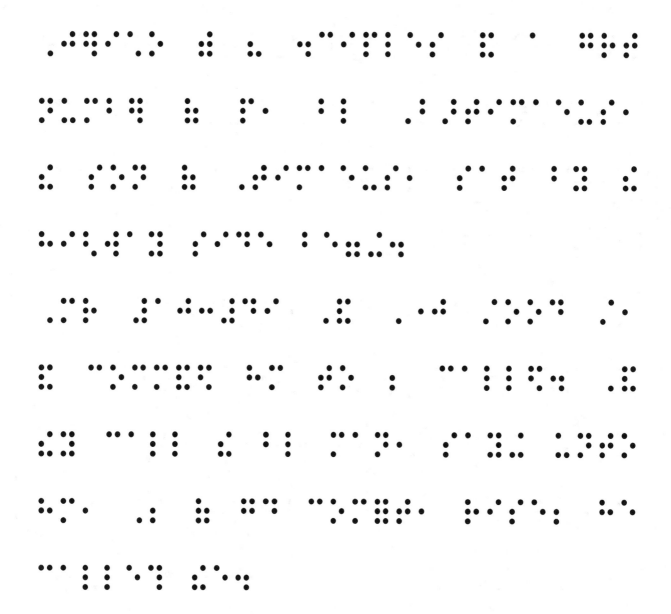

EXERCISE 22.2 D

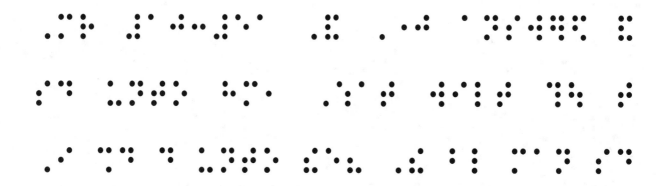

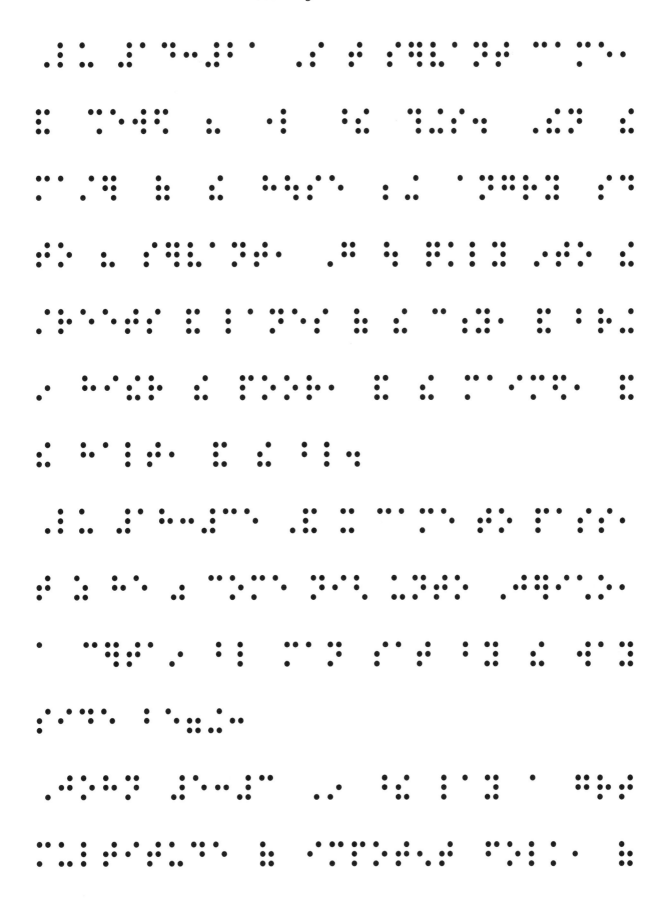

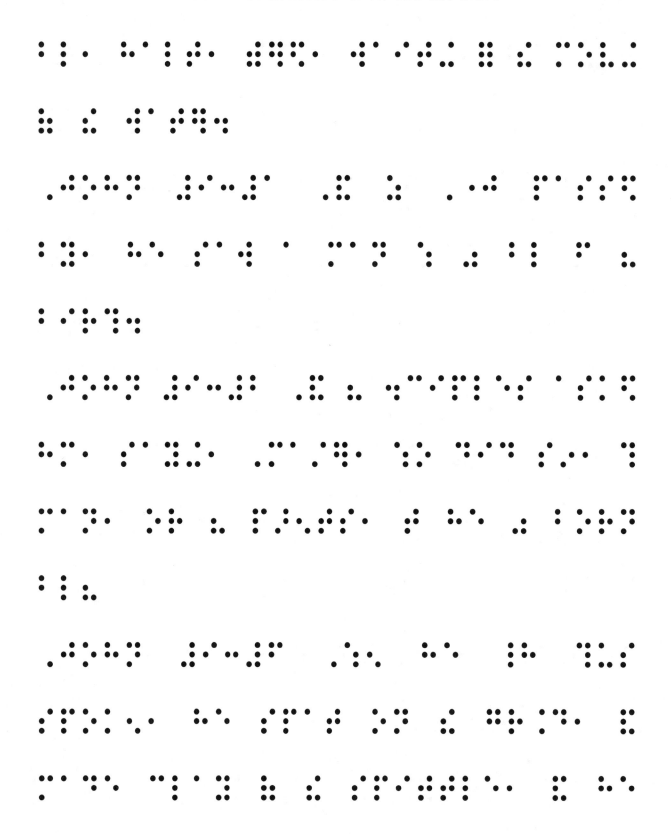

EXERCISE 22.2 E

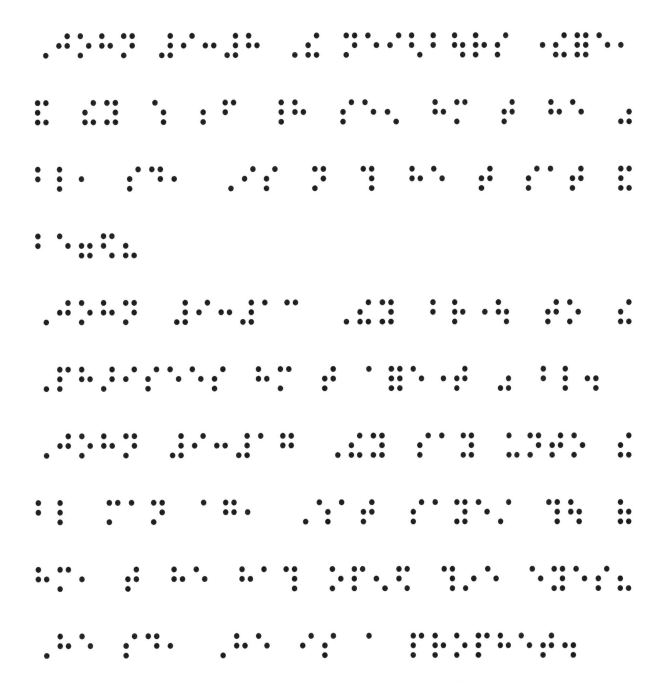

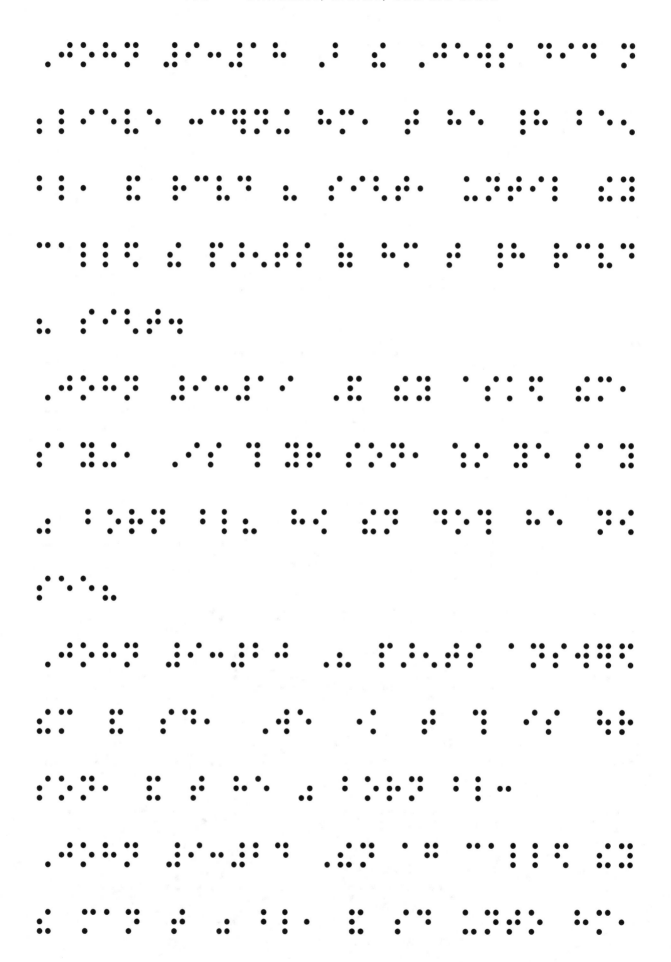

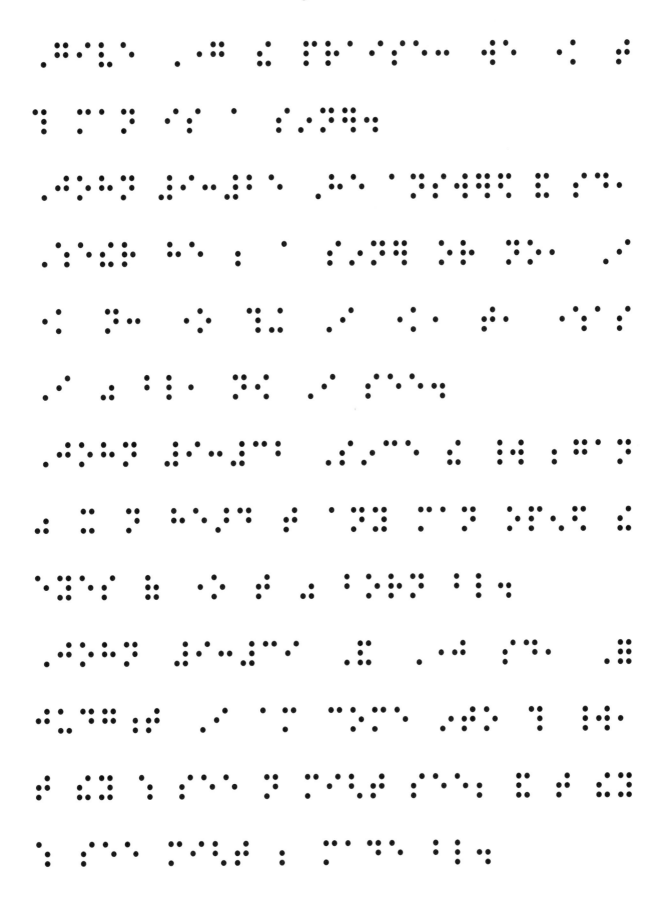

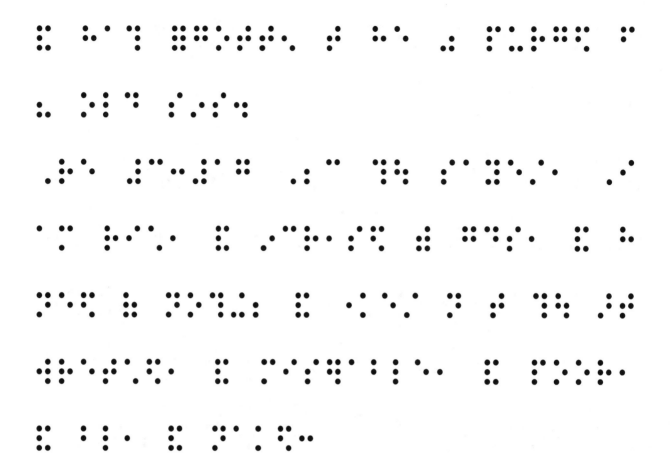

Lesson 23: Font Changes

Italic Indicator

⠘⠆	Italic symbol indicator
⠘⠂	Italic word indicator
⠘⠶	Italic passage indicator
⠘⠄	Italic terminator

- Italic symbol: Dots 4 6, 2 3 are brailled immediately before a single italicized letter.
- Italicized word: Dots 4 6, 2 are brailled immediately prior to an italicized word.
- Italicized passage: Dots 4 6, 2 3 5 6 are brailled immediately prior to the first word in the italicized passage. The passage is terminated by the italic terminator sign—dots 4 6, 3—after the final italicized word.
- The italic indicator is brailled immediately prior to a letter or word to indicate that it is in italic in the print copy.

Examples:

Bright	⠘⠂⠃⠗⠊⠛⠓⠞
The Times	⠘⠶⠠⠹⠑⠀⠠⠞⠊⠍⠑⠎⠘⠄
1939-1945	⠘⠶⠼⠁⠊⠉⠊⠤⠼⠁⠊⠙⠑⠘⠄

- When three or more consecutive words in the print copy are printed in italic, the italic passage indicator is brailled immediately prior to the first word. The italic terminator sign is placed after the last italicized word and before the next space, hyphen, dash, or oblique stroke.

Example:

Three or more words	⠘⠶⠹⠗⠑⠑⠀⠕⠗⠀⠍⠕⠗⠑⠀⠺⠕⠗⠙⠎⠘⠄

- The scope of the italic passage indicator extends to all words or letters that follow it until the italic terminator sign is reached, regardless of the italicized passage's length and whether it spans multiple pages.
- In an italicized passage, the first word of each paragraph must be preceded by the italicized passage indicator but the italic terminator sign is not written until after the final word of the final paragraph.

- Compound words joined by a hyphen, such as "sea-lion," "up-to-date," and "co-ordinate," are treated as if they were a single word. This means that the italic word indicator is placed at the beginning of the hyphenated sequence and naturally terminated at the space. Italicized dates are treated in the same way.

Example:

1914-18

- In phrases of more than two italicized words joined by hyphens, the italic word indicator must precede the first word and is terminated by the space.

Example:

out-of-the-way

- Abbreviations such as "i.e." or "e.g.," which are written in one undivided group, need only one italic indicator.

Example:

e.g.

- When several italicized book titles are listed one after the other, each title must be italicized separately.

Example:

More than Meets the Eye, If a Picture Paints a Thousand Words, The Sufficiency of Scripture, etc., are some of the titles by Joseph Stephen.

- The use of the italic indicator does not change the rules regarding any lower group- or wordsigns. The examples cited in the lessons on lowersigns are brailled the same way regardless of the italic indicator. For example: <u>be</u> were his was enough in, which must be spaced from other signs, may be used even though they are immediately preceded by the italic indicator. Similarly, just because an italic indicator is used immediately prior to a lower symbol does not make that symbol's usage legal if it would not be so without the indicator's presence.

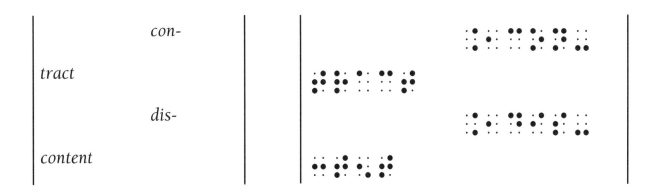

	con-		
tract			
	dis-		
content			

The Part-Word Italic Sign

When part of a word—more than one character—is printed in italics, the italicized part must be preceded by the italic word indicator " ⠨⠨ " and followed by the italic termination indicator " ⠨⠄ ".

Examples:

*ab*solutely

abso*lutely*

Bold and Underline

Symbols also exist for indicating bold and underlined text and are shown here without example or exercise. Their usage is basically identical to that of the italic indicators.

```
Bold Indicator

⠘⠆ Bold symbol indicator
⠘⠂ Bold word indicator
⠘⠶ Bold passage indicator
⠘⠄ Bold terminator
```

- Bold symbol: Dots 4 5, 2 3 must precede a single bold letter.
- Bold word: Dots 4 5, 2 must precede a bolded word.
- Bold passage: Dots 4 5, 2 3 5 6 must precede a bold passage. The bold passage must be terminated by the bold terminator symbol, dots 4 5, 3. ~'

```
Underline Indicator

⠸⠆ Underline symbol indicator
⠸⠂ Underline word indicator
⠸⠶ Underline passage indicator
⠸⠄ Underline terminator
```

- Underlined symbol: Dots 4 5 6, 2 3 must precede a single underlined letter.
- Underlined word: Dots 4 5 6, 2 must precede an underlined word.
- Underlined passage: Dots 4 5 6, 2 3 5 6 must precede an underlined passage. The underlined passage is terminated by the underline terminator symbol, dots 4 5 6, 3. ⠸⠄

EXERCISE 23.1

Now that you have learned italics in Scripture, transcribe the verse below using symbols for italics.

Note: There is a Braille symbol for paragraph marks, but since it is not used in the Braille Bible, we will not use it here.

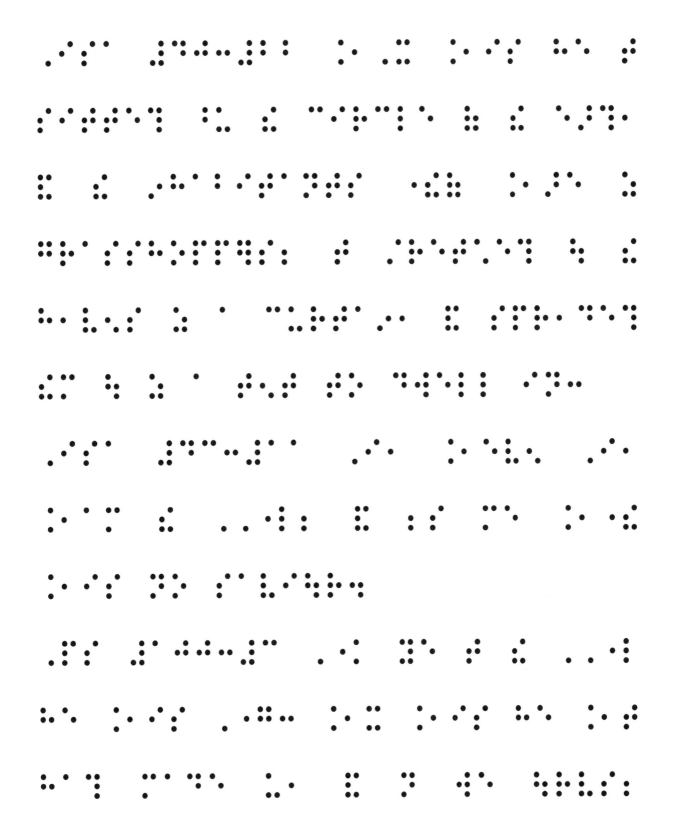

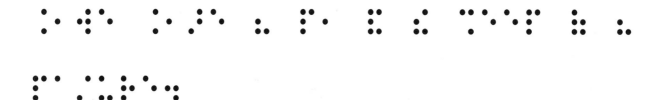

Exercise 23.2 A

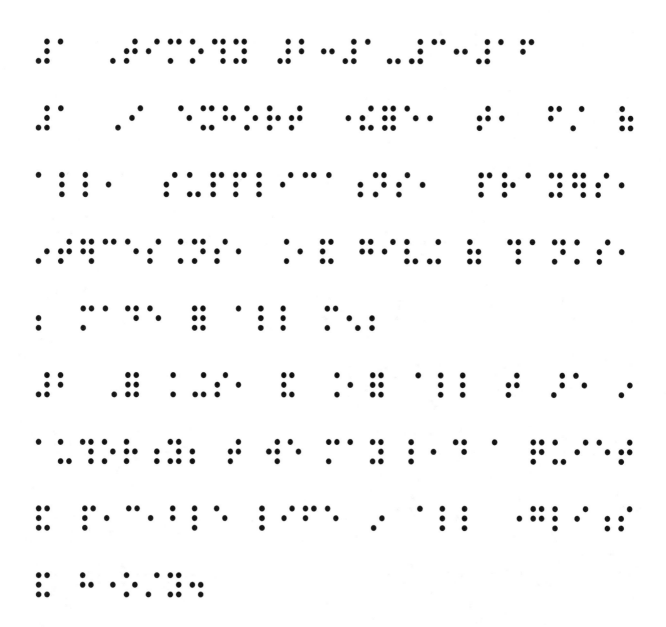

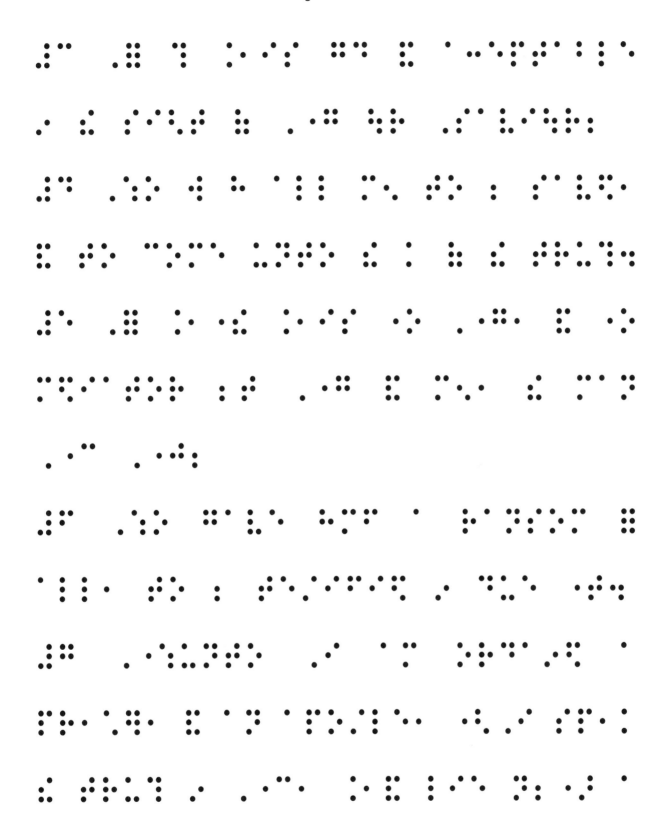

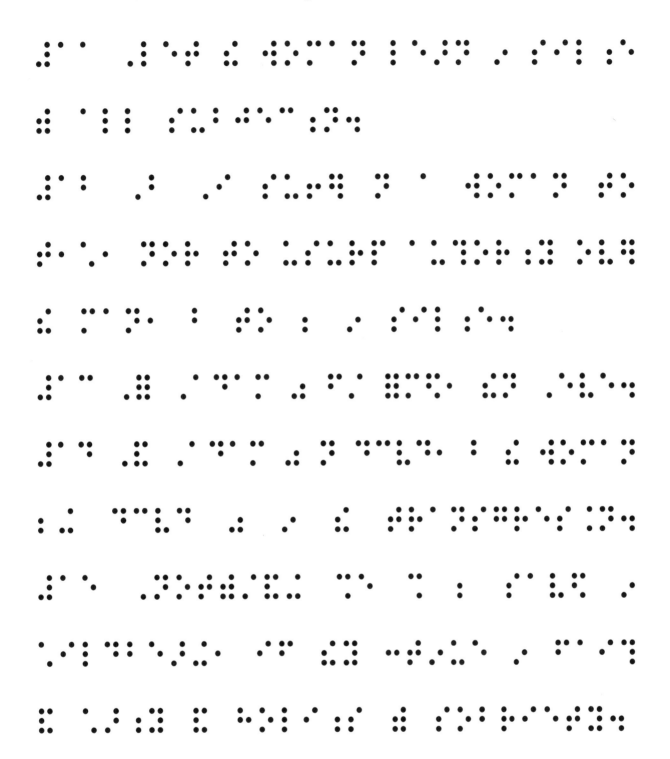

EXERCISE 23.2 B

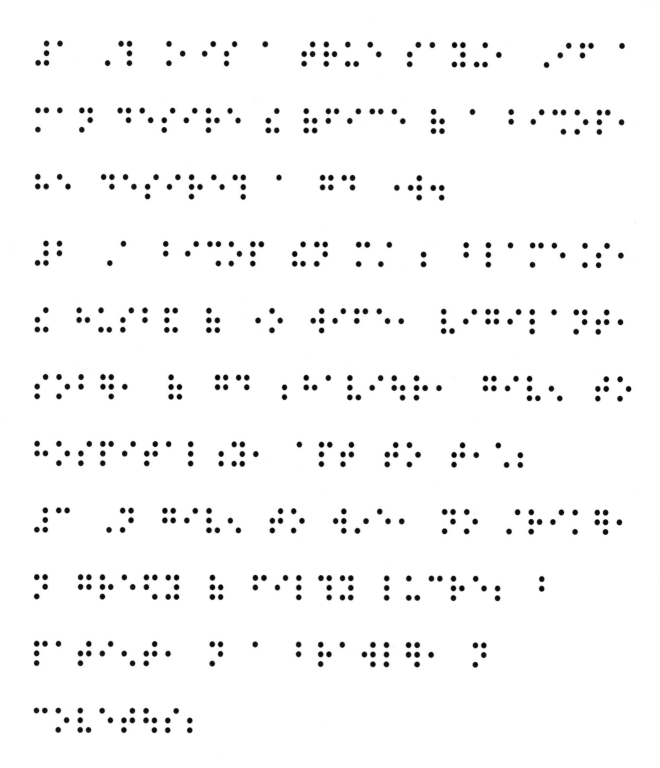

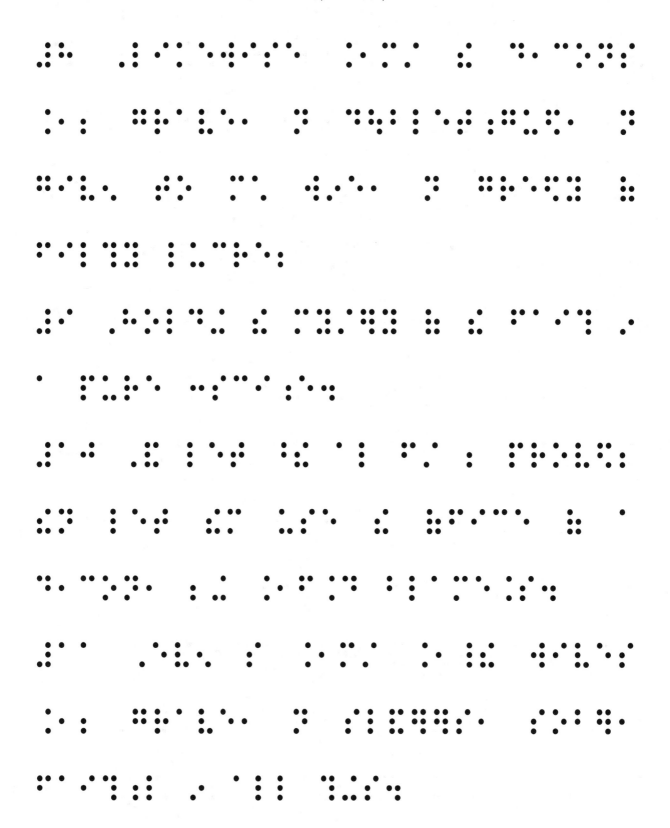

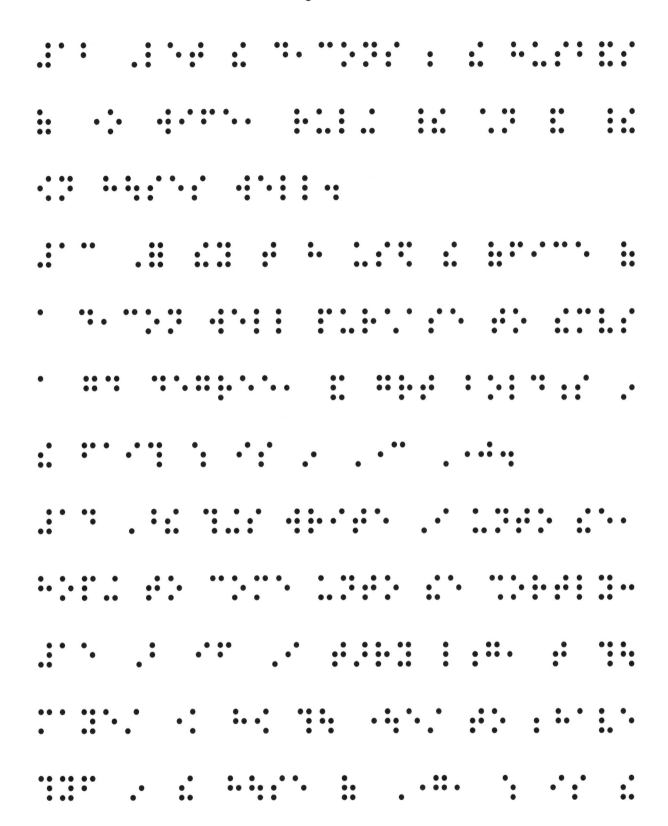

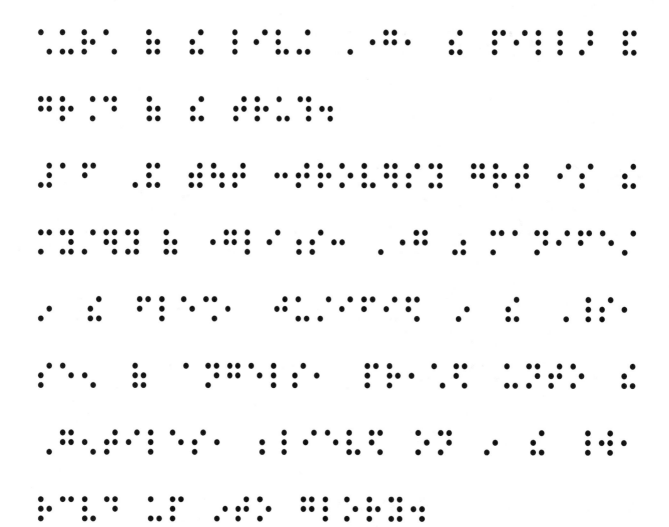

Conclusion

THIS BOOK INTRODUCES many of the Unified Braille Code symbols. We have been brief on the rules because Braille is incredibly complex—as you may now appreciate. For the complete up-to-date rules, please visit http://www.iceb.org/ueb.html.

We hope that this book has given you an appreciation for what many blind people must overcome just to be able to read and write, let alone be employed, have a family, or excel in any field. As Christians, we have much to learn about providing assistance to the disabled and taking seriously the Lord Jesus' injunction in Luke 14:13-14 to help those without expectation.

We also hope this book has given you an empathy for the difficulties blind people face in their everyday lives. There is so much we all take for granted—may we be truly grateful for the five senses with which the Lord has endowed us. Yet even blind people who lack one of these senses can be grateful that they have the other four senses and can still glorify God with their lives as they depend more entirely on His grace to live.

> But when thou makest a feast,
> call the poor, the maimed, the lame, the blind:
> And thou shalt be blessed;
> for they cannot recompense thee:
> for thou shalt be recompensed at the resurrection of the just.
>
> Luke 14:13-14

Common Terms Relating to Blindness and Vision Impairment

20/20 Vision—A measurement of visual acuity (or clearness of sight) that most eye-care professionals consider as the mean. The level of acuity is routinely measured by requiring an individual to identify various sizes of black symbols on a white background at a distance—an eye chart. The first numeral 20 defines the distance in feet from the individual. The second numeral 20 defines the distance from which a person can distinguish characters on an eye chart that is 20 feet away. Most people can identify characters on an eye chart at 20 feet. A person with 20/10 eyesight can see at 20 feet what a person with normal sight (20/20) can see when standing 10 feet away.

Accessible Pocket PC—A portable notetaker device that provides the blind and those with other levels of vision loss with the features and functionality afforded to sighted people who use mainstream PDAs (see "notetaker").

AMD—AMD is an acronym for Age-related Macular Degeneration, characterized by a worsening loss of central vision as a result of deterioration of the macula, which contains retinal cones required for sight.

Amsler Grid—A black-lined grid on a white background used for testing central-sight field distortion and impairments that signal macular degeneration and other vision loss issues.

Aqueous Humor—the clear fluid contained between the iris and cornea that provides necessary nutrients to the lens and cornea. When this fluid cannot drain, it creates unrelieved pressure that can result in glaucoma and vision loss.

Asteroid Hyalosis—A situation that results in moving spots or flecks ("floaters") that affect clear vision, which is a result of particles of calcium-rich fat that becomes suspended in the vitreous.

Astigmatism—An eye disorder caused by uneven curvature of the eyeball that motivates light rays to bend, targeting more than one point of the retina instead of a single spot. This causes blurry vision, vague shadows on characters when reading, and slight double vision.

Blepharospasm—A condition that causes involuntary blinking to an excessive measure that the affected individual cannot see. Blepharospasm is considered as a form of functional blindness.

Braille—A tactile reading and writing system invented by Louis Braille in the 1820's and widely used by the blind and deaf-blind. Braille is made up of a system of raised dots felt with the fingertips. Braille makes reading, writing, note-taking, and communicating possible for blind and deaf-blind users.

Braille Display—A tactile device consisting of a row of rectangular cells, each of which contains a series of moveable pins. The pins are controlled electronically to move up or down to form Braille characters. The characters depict the information that appears on the text source, typically via a computer or notetaker device.

Cataracts—Caused by aging in conjunction with diabetes, excessive exposure to UV rays, or smoking and excessive steroid use, cataracts result in clouding or yellowing of the eye lens, which creates blurred vision, halos around objects (lights, in particular), glare, and diminished perception of color saturation.

CCTV/Closed-circuit television—a video camera system that broadcasts a signal to a specific monitor (as opposed to a public broadcast source). Video magnifiers for low-vision users are sometimes referred to as CCTVs.

Central Serous Retinopathy—A vision-loss condition that usually results in blurred or distorted central vision caused by fluid collecting under the macula.

CMV Retinitis—A visual impairment characterized by spots before the eyes (floaters) and blurred and/or distorted vision. Commonly experienced by people with immune deficiencies.

Contrast Sensitivity—A property that regulates the level at which the eye can detect differences in contrast between an object or character and its background—for instance, the contrast between black printed letters and the white page on which they appear.

Corneal Dystrophy—Classified under several categories, corneal dystrophy is a medical syndrome that results in loss of transparency of the cornea. Individuals who have this condition experience differing levels of blurred vision, light sensitivity, and vision loss.

Diabetic Retinopathy— The leading cause of vision loss in people who are diagnosed with diabetes. Diabetic retinopathy is brought on by leakage of the retinal blood vessels and can develop into progressive blurred vision, double vision, floaters, visual distortion, and ultimately some degree of blindness.

Floaters/Spots—see Asteroid Hyalosis

Glaucoma—A sight impairment caused by unrelieved pressure inside the eye as a result of fluid build-up. Permanent impairment can range from loss of peripheral vision to severe vision loss. Individuals with glaucoma may experience increased frequency of headaches, blurred vision, halos around lights, difficulty seeing in the dark, and sometimes a non-reactive pupil, pain, or swollen eye.

Grave's Disease—An autoimmune disorder that occurs due to thyroid abnormality. Grave's Disease can affect vision, including eye discomfort, double vision, and degrees of vision loss.

Hyperiopia/Hyperopic/Farsighted—A person is considered "farsighted," when items at a distance are in focus but close object are blurry. The medical term for farsightedness is *hyperiopia*.

Keratoconus—An eye disorder that leads to degeneration of vision and various degrees of vision loss, ranging from blurred, doubled, or distorted vision to severe vision loss that cannot be improved with glasses or other common optical aids. Keratoconus results from a severe form of astigmatism in which the cornea thins and reforms into a cone-shaped bulge.

Legally Blind—Having 20/200 vision in the best eye with correction or a visual field of 20 degrees or less.

Low Vision—A significant reduction of visual acuity that ordinary eyeglasses, contact lenses, and/or medical treatment cannot completely correct.

Macula—The small area in the retina that contains special cells that are especially sensitive to light. The macula enables people to see fine details clearly.

Macular Degeneration—see AMD

Metamorphopsia—Distorted vision caused by impairments of the eye's macula and/or retina. Objects may look nearer or farther than they really are, and lines may appear wavy or bent.

Multiple-view magnification camera—A portable, rotating closed-circuit camera that provides magnified views of objects from varying distances — from close-up self-view magnification, to document views for reading, to the magnification of objects from across large rooms or auditoriums.

Myopia/Myopic/Nearsighted—A person is considered nearsighted or myopic when close-up items are in focus but more distant objects are blurry, by degree.

Notetaker—A portable electronic Braille device that enables blind users to take notes, create documents, and access applications. These devices usually provide either speech or Braille output or both. See Accessible Pocket PC.

OCR/Optical Character Recognition—Electronic conversion of images or printed text into machine-editable, readable text after capture by scanning.

Ocular Albinism—A condition in which lack of pigmentation in the eye results in light sensitivity, blurry vision, and varying degrees of vision loss.

Presbyopia—An eye disorder of middle age, usually first evidenced by some minor loss of vision, such as blurred letters while reading at a normal close-up distance. Clear vision degenerates over time into more significant loss of near sight as the individual continues to age. It could be caused by loss of the eye's natural lens elasticity.

Retinal Detachment—A critical eye condition in which the retina—the part of the eye that receives light and translates it into signals that allow the brain to form images—separates from the underlying tissue. Some people experience floaters, shadows over vision, very blurred vision, and/or unexplained flashes of light. Without immediate treatment, permanent damage may occur, including significant vision loss to blindness. Retinal detachment is most commonly found in people who are older, have severe myopia, have had cataract surgery, or have been diagnosed with diabetic retinopathy.

Retinitis Pigmentosa—a progressive visual impairment with various end-results ranging from significant vision loss to total blindness. Symptoms include night blindness and loss of peripheral vision. Retinitis pigmentosa is one of the most common forms of inherited retinal degeneration.

Scanning and Reading—A means to convert text to speech output and computer screen text via OCR and speech software.

Screen Magnification Software—Software that interfaces with a computer's graphical output to present enlarged images of monitor content.

Screen Reader—Software, such as JAWS, that interprets computer screen content and reads it aloud via synchronized speech.

Speech Synthesizer—Software that works with a computer's sound card to produce speech.

Video Magnifier—A means of enlarging the appearance of text and images via a closed-circuit video camera system by projecting magnified views from a camera's field of focus to a computer monitor (see CCTV).

Visual Acuity—See 20/20 Vision

Video Magnification—See Video Magnifier

Visual Field—A measurement based on the width of the panorama an individual can see. The normal human visual field extends to approximately 60 degrees inward toward the nose and each eye, to 100 degrees outward away from the nose, and approximately 60 degrees above and 75 below the horizontal meridian.

Braille Reference

Table of Braille Signs

Line 1 (dots 1 2 4 5)

a   b   c   d   e   f   g   h   i   j

Line 2 (line 1 + dot 3)

k   l   m   n   o   p   q   r   s   t

Line 3 (line 1 + dots 3 6)

u   v   x   y   z   and   for   of   the   with

Line 4 (line 1 + dot 6)

ch   gh   sh   th   wh   ed   er   ou   ow   w

Line 5 (line 1 lowered)

	be	con	dis	en				"	in
ea	bb	cc				ff	gg		
,	;	:	.			!		?	"
	be	ratio sign	decimal point	enough			were	his	in	was

Line 6 (dot 3 with dots 4 5 6)

st   ing   numeric indicator   ar   '   -

Line 7 (dots 4 5 6)

accent sign   line sign   italic indicator   grade 1 indicator   capital sign

composite contraction prefixes

Upper Contractions

Sign	Word Sign Standing alone	Initial Contractions With Dot 5	With Dots 4-5	With Dots 4-5-6	Final Contractions With Dots 4-6	With Dots 5-6
⠁	a	...	...	...		...
⠃	but	...	...	...		...
⠉	can	Christ	...	cannot		...
⠙	do	day	...	...		...
⠑	every	ever	...	...		ence
⠋	from	father	...	...		...
⠛	go	God	...	...		ong
⠓	have	here	...	had		...
⠊	i	...	...	...		...
⠚	just	Jesus	...	...		...
⠅	knowledge	know	...	...		...
⠇	like	lord	...	...		ful
⠍	more	mother	...	many		...
⠝	not	name	...	...		tion
⠕	o	one	...	...		...
⠏	people	part	...	...		...
⠟	quite	question	...	...		...
⠗	rather	right	...	...		...
⠎	so	some	...	spirit		ness
⠞	that	time	...	...		ment
⠥	us	under	upon	...		...
⠧	very	...	...	...		...
⠺	will	work	word	world		...
⠭	it	...	...	...		...
⠽	you	young	...	...		ity
⠵	as	...	...	...		...

Sign	Group-sign	Wordsign Standing alone	Initial Contractions With Dot 5	With Dots 4-5	With Dots 4-5-6
		and	...	...	...
		for	...	...	...
		of	...	...	...
		the	there	these	their
		with	...	...	...
	ch	child	character	...	...
	gh	...	...	...	...
	sh	shall	...	...	...
	th	this	through	those	...
	wh	which	where	whose	...
	ed	...	...	...	...
	er	...	...	...	...
	ou	out	ought	...	...
	ow	...	...	...	...
	st	still	...	...	...
	ar	...	...	...	...
	ing	...	...	...	...

Lower Contractions

Sign	Wordsign	Groupsign/Punctuation Start of word	Middle of word	End of word
	...	...	ea	,
	be	be	bb	;
	...	con	cc	:
	...	dis	...	.
	...	...	-	-
	enough	en	en	en
	...	...	ff	!
	were	...	gg	...
	his	"	...	?
	was	...	...	"
	in	in	in	in

SHORTFORMS

Word	Short	Word	Short	Word	Short
about	ab	conceive	concv	ourselves	ourvs
above	abv	conceiving	concvg	paid	pd
according	ac	could	cd	perceive	percv
across	acr	deceive	dcv	perceiving	percvg
after	af	deceiving	dcvg	perhaps	perh
afternoon	afn	declare	dcl	quick	qk
afterward	afw	declaring	dclg	receive	rcv
again	ag	either	ei	receiving	rcvg
against	agst	first	fst	rejoice	rjc
almost	alm	friend	fr	rejoicing	rjcg
already	alr	good	gd	said	sd
also	al	great	grt	should	shd
although	alth	herself	herf	such	sch
altogether	alt	him	hm	themselves	themvs
always	alw	himself	hmf	thyself	thyf
because	bec	immediate	imm	today	td
before	bef	its	xs	together	tgr
behind	beh	itself	xf	tomorrow	tm
below	bel	letter	lr	tonight	tn
beneath	ben	little	ll	would	wd
beside	bes	much	mch	your	yr
between	bet	must	mst	yourself	yrf
beyond	bey	myself	myf	yourselves	yrvs
blind	bl	necessary	nec		
Braille	Brl	neither	nei		
children	chn	oneself	onef		

Braille Signs

A

a

-ance

and

ar

as

At Sign @

Asterisk *

(a)

B

b

bb

be

but

Bold Symbol

Bold Word

Bold Passage

Bold Terminator

(b)

C

c

can

cannot

Capital Sign

Capital Word

Capital Passage

Capital Terminator

cc

ch

character

child

Christ

con

(c)

D

d

Dagger †

(d)

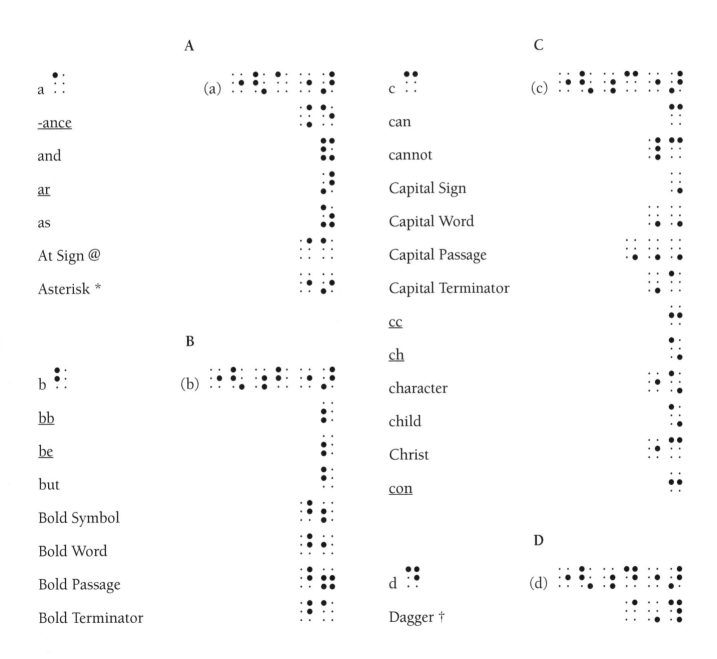

day		for	
Decimal Point		from	
Degree Sign		-ful	
dis			
Ditto Sign			
Division Sign		**G**	
do		g	
Dollar Sign $		gg	
Double Dagger		gh	
		God	
E		go	
e		**H**	
ea		h	
ed		had	
en		have	
-ence		here	
enough		his	
Equals Sign			
er		**I**	
Euro Sign		i	
ever		in	
every		ing	
		it	
F		Italic Symbol	
f		Italic Word	
father		Italic Passage	
ff		Italic Terminator	
		-ity	

J

j

Jesus

just

K

k

know

knowledge

L

l

-less

like

Line Sign

lord

M

m

many

-ment

Minus Sign

more

mother

Multiplication Sign

N

n

name

-ness

not

Numeric Indicator

O

o

Oblique Stroke /

of

-ong

one

ou

ought

-ound

-ount

out

ow

P

p

¶ Paragraph Sign

part

people

% Per Cent Sign

Plus Sign

Pound Sign £

Punctuation

- Apostrophe '
- Round Bracket ( )
- Square Bracket [ ]
- Colon :
- Comma ,
- Dash —
- Long Dash ———
- Long Dash ---- ----
- Ellipsis …
- Exclamation !
- Full Stop .
- Hyphen -
- Query ?
- Outer Quotes
- Inner Quotes
- Semi-colon ;

Q

- q
- question
- quite

R

- r
- rather
- right

S

- s
- Section Sign §
- sh
- shall
- -sion
- so
- some
- spirit
- st
- still

T

- t
- th
- that
- the
- their
- there
- these
- this
- those
- through
- time
- -tion

Transcriber's brackets	
(open)	⠈⠨⠣
(close)	⠈⠨⠜

U

u	⠥
under	⠐⠥
Underline Symbol	⠸⠆
Underline Word	⠸⠂
Underline Passage	⠸⠶
Underline Terminator	⠸⠁
upon	⠘⠥
us	⠥

V

v	⠧
very	⠧

W

w	⠺
was	⠴
were	⠶
<u>wh</u>	⠱
where	⠐⠱
which	⠱
whose	⠘⠱
will	⠺
with	⠾
word	⠘⠺
work	⠐⠺
world	⠸⠺

X

x	⠭

Y

y	⠽
you	⠽
young	⠐⠽

Z

z	⠵

Answers

Detach answer key by placing thumb on first page and forefinger behind last page of answers pullling carefully from top to bottom to detach from spine.

Exercise 1

1. C. Allow them to hold you just above the elbow.
2. B. Allow them to find the obstacle with their cane (unless it is dangerous).
3. C. Introduce yourself by name and talk naturally; gently touch them on the shoulder if they do not realize you are talking to them.
4. A. Politely excuse yourself.
5. A. Ask if they'd like you to describe where their food is, using a clock face for reference.
6. B. Stop at the stairs, inform them that there are ascending or descending stairs, and place their hand on the handrail.
7. C. Have varying amounts of sight from nothing to reasonable vision, depending on their eye condition.
8. A. They may think you have gone away and need reassurance that you're still there.
9. A. Announce your presence and announce who is with you.
10. C. Be sensitive to the needs of both the blind and sighted parent. The sighted parent will have an extra responsibility and burden to ensure that both their blind spouse and children are taken care of.

Exercise 1.1

aid acid ace acacia add abide age bad bed big beige cab cage chief chide decide deaf die dig dice ebb egg edge feed fig face fife jagged head hid heed hi ice if idea jade jig

Exercise 1.2

children made seat jest good soon map bride rod oats fond load snap glad rock me tip take nod ripe see let soap road meet same sale lame moss poll nose rattle command metal float inspire born again important home able tomb ham kettle man camp gold bird rope jams bang fold mile animal ask seek knock thank

EXERCISE 1.3

azure axe veil tree ark mountain altar worship saviour kindness faith hope charity victory patient peace love joy hope gold silver precious stones live eternity favour quiver govern self control people heaven hold equity judgment exist follow after that which is good evening morning day night helper soul spirit fruit vine abide qualify accepted beloved behaviour mission zeal holy godly

EXERCISE 2.1

(A) 27	(B) 300	(C) 60
(D) 969	(E) 1	(F) 119
(G) 12	(H) 120	(I) 130
(J) 15	(K) 150	(L) 1656
(M) 17	(N) 175	(O) 176
(P) 180	(Q) 10	(R) 100
(S) 2	(T) 20	(U) 3
(V) 39	(W) 30	(X) 4
(Y) 40	(Z) 5	(AA) 50
(BB) 6	(CC) 66	(DD) 600
(EE) 7	(FF) 75	(GG) 8
(HH) 99		

EXERCISE 2.2

(a) CC (b) V (c) A (d) E; S; U; X; Z; BB; EE (e) D
(f) L (g) B; W; AA; E; E; U (h) EE; S (i) U (j) GG
(k) Y; J (l) K; EE; M (m) Q; Q; E (n) Y (o) EE
(p) EE (q) DD; E; E; E (r) S; EE; T (s) R; HH (t) Y
(u) C (v) N (w) FF; J; G; E; P; H (x) I
(y) G (z) K; F; O

(a) Books in the Bible: 66
(b) Books in the Old Testament: 39
(c) Books in the New Testament: 27
(d) On day 1 of creation God divided the light from the darkness.
    On day 2 of creation, God made the sky.
    On day 3 of creation, God made land and sea and all plants.
    On day 4 of creation, God made the sun, moon, and stars.

On day <u>5</u> of creation, God made sea creatures and birds.

On day <u>6</u> of creation, God made land animals and man.

On day <u>7</u> of creation, God rested from all His work.

(e) And all the days of Methuselah were <u>969</u> years.

(f) From creation to flood was <u>1656</u> years

(g) Noah was commanded to build an ark <u>300</u> cubits long by <u>30</u> cubits high by <u>50</u> cubits wide. There was <u>1</u> window in it <u>1</u> cubit from the top. There were <u>3</u> stories.

(h) Noah was commanded to bring <u>7</u> of each clean animal and <u>2</u> of each unclean animal into the ark.

(i) Noah had <u>3</u> sons.

(j) There were <u>8</u> people on the ark.

(k) It rained for <u>40</u> days.

The waters were <u>15</u> cubits above the tallest mountain.

(l) The waters prevailed upon the earth <u>150</u> days.

The ark rested in the <u>7</u>th month, on the <u>17</u>th day of the month, upon the mountains of Ararat.

(m) The waters decreased continually until the <u>10</u>th month; in the <u>10</u>th month, on the <u>1</u>st day of the month, were the tops of the mountains seen.

(n) Noah waited another <u>40</u> days before he let a raven and a dove go out the window.

(o) After the dove returned, he waited another <u>7</u> days and let the dove go again.

(p) After the dove returned with an olive leaf, he waited yet another <u>7</u> days.

(q) In the <u>600</u>th and <u>1</u>st year, in the <u>1</u>st month, the <u>1</u>st day of the month, the waters were dried up from off the earth: and Noah removed the covering of the ark, and looked, and behold, the face of the ground was dry.

(r) In the <u>2</u>nd month, on the <u>7</u> and <u>20</u>th day of the month, was the earth dried.

(s) Abraham had Isaac when he was <u>100</u> years old and Sarah was <u>99</u>.

(t) Isaac married Rebekah when he was <u>40</u> years old.

(u) Jacob was born when Isaac was <u>60</u> years old.

(v) Abraham died when he was <u>175</u> years old.

(w) When Abraham died, Isaac was <u>75</u> and Jacob was <u>15</u>.

Jacob had <u>12</u> sons and <u>1</u> daughter (that we know of).

Isaac died at <u>180</u> years old. When he died, Jacob was <u>120</u> years old.

(x) Jacob was <u>130</u> years old when he stood before Pharaoh. He died soon after that.

(y) There were <u>12</u> apostles.

(z) There are <u>150</u> Psalms and the longest is <u>119</u> with <u>176</u> verses.

EXERCISE 3.1

Jeremiah 9:23 and 24

<u>Thus</u> saith the <u>LORD</u>, <u>Let</u> not the wise man glory in his wisdom, neither let the mighty man glory in his might, let not the rich man glory in his riches:

<u>But</u> let him that glorieth glory in this, that he understandeth and knoweth me, that <u>I</u> am the <u>LORD</u> which exercise lovingkindness, judgment, and righteousness, in the earth: for in these things <u>I</u> delight, saith the <u>LORD</u>.

EXERCISE 3.2

1 Corinthians 1:26-31

For ye see your calling, brethren, how that not many wise men after the flesh, not many mighty, not many noble, are called:

But God hath chosen the foolish things of the world to confound the wise; and God hath chosen the weak things of the world to confound the things which are mighty;

And base things of the world, and things which are despised, hath God chosen, yea, and things which are not, to bring to nought things that are:

That no flesh should glory in his presence.

But of him are ye in Christ Jesus, who of God is made unto us wisdom, and righteousness, and sanctification, and redemption:

That, according as it is written, He that glorieth, let him glory in the Lord.

EXERCISE 3.3

Thou shalt not curse the deaf nor put a stumbling block before the blind but shalt fear thy God I am the LORD Leviticus chapter 19 verse 14

EXERCISE 4.1

Note: Answers are underlined

Revelation 4:11
Thou art worthy, O Lord, to receive glory <u>and</u> honour <u>and</u> power; <u>for</u> thou hast created all things, <u>and</u> <u>for</u> thy pleasure they were, <u>and</u> are created.

Mark 8:38
Whosoever therefore shall be ashamed <u>of</u> me <u>and</u> <u>of</u> my words in this adulterous <u>and</u> sinful generation; <u>of</u> him also shall <u>the</u> Son <u>of</u> man be ashamed, when he cometh in <u>the</u> glory <u>of</u> his Father <u>with</u> <u>the</u> holy angels.

Luke 12:8

Also I say unto you, Whosoever shall confess me before men, him shall <u>the</u> Son <u>of</u> man also confess before the angels of God:

Exercise 5.1

Proverbs 1:7

<u>The</u> fear <u>of</u> <u>the</u> <u>LORD</u> is <u>the</u> beginning <u>of</u> <u>knowledge</u>: <u>but</u> fools despise wisdom <u>and</u> instruction.

Matthew 4:4

<u>But</u> he answered <u>and</u> said, <u>It</u> is written, Man shall <u>not</u> live by bread alone, <u>but</u> by <u>every</u> word <u>that</u> proceedeth out <u>of</u> <u>the</u> mouth <u>of</u> <u>God</u>.

Genesis 1:31

<u>And</u> <u>God</u> saw <u>every</u> thing <u>that</u> he had made, <u>and</u>, behold, <u>it</u> was <u>very</u> good. <u>And</u> <u>the</u> evening <u>and</u> <u>the</u> morning were <u>the</u> sixth day.

Proverbs 16:16

<u>How</u> much better is <u>it</u> to get wisdom than gold! <u>and</u> to get understanding <u>rather</u> to be chosen than silver!

Exodus 23:24

<u>Thou</u> shalt <u>not</u> bow down to their gods, nor serve them, nor <u>do</u> after their works: <u>but</u> thou shalt utterly overthrow them, <u>and</u> <u>quite</u> break down their images.

Psalm 56:4

In <u>God</u> <u>I</u> <u>will</u> praise his word, in <u>God</u> <u>I</u> <u>have</u> put my trust; <u>I</u> <u>will</u> <u>not</u> fear what flesh <u>can</u> <u>do</u> unto me.

2 Timothy 3:15

<u>And</u> <u>that</u> <u>from</u> <u>a</u> child thou hast known <u>the</u> holy scriptures, which are able to make thee wise unto salvation through faith which is in <u>Christ</u> <u>Jesus</u>.

1 Corinthians 6:1

Dare any <u>of</u> <u>you</u>, having <u>a</u> matter against another, <u>go</u> to law before <u>the</u> unjust, <u>and</u> <u>not</u> before <u>the</u> saints?

Deuteronomy 32:4

He is the Rock, his work is perfect: for all his ways are judgment: a God of truth and without iniquity, just and right is he.

1 Samuel 2:2
There is none holy as the LORD: for there is none beside thee: neither is there any rock like our God.

Psalm 92:10
But my horn shalt thou exalt like the horn of an unicorn: I shall be anointed with fresh oil.

John 16:21
A woman when she is in travail hath sorrow, because her hour is come: but as soon as she is delivered of the child, she remembereth no more the anguish, for joy that a man is born into the world.

1 Corinthians 10:7
Neither be ye idolaters, as were some of them; as it is written, The people sat down to eat and drink, and rose up to play.

1 Peter 1:15
But as he which hath called you is holy, so be ye holy in all manner of conversation;

Genesis 1:26
And God said, Let us make man in our image, after our likeness: and let them have dominion over the fish of the sea, and over the fowl of the air, and over the cattle, and over all the earth, and over every creeping thing that creepeth upon the earth.

EXERCISE 6.1

1 A Song of degrees for Solomon. Except the LORD build the house, they labour in vain that build it: except the LORD keep the city, the watchman waketh but in vain.

2 It is vain for you to rise up early, to sit up late, to eat the bread of sorrows: for so he giveth his beloved sleep.

3 Lo, children are an heritage of the LORD: and the fruit of the womb is his reward.

4 As arrows are in the hand of a mighty man; so are children of the youth.

5 Happy is the man that hath his quiver full of them: they shall not be ashamed, but they shall speak with the enemies in the gate.

EXERCISE 6.2

The prophet Amos said, "Hate the evil and love the good." God hates evil! The Lord's mercy is toward them that fear him. Do you fear the Lord?

EXERCISE 7.1

Proverbs 23:17 ⠿ LORD ⠿ day

Proverbs 12:19 ⠿ ever

Mark 6:3 ⠿ here

Proverbs 4:1 ⠿ father ⠿ know

Proverbs 18:10 ⠿ name ⠿ LORD

Proverbs 15:12 ⠿ one

1 Peter 4:14 ⠿ name ⠿ Christ ⠿ God ⠿ part ⠿ part

1 Corinthians 10:27 ⠿ question

Proverbs 4:16 ⠿ some

Proverbs 25:19 ⠿ time

Proverbs 12:24 ⠿ under

Proverbs 20:11 ⠿ work ⠿ right.

Proverbs 30:17 ⠿ father ⠿ mother ⠿ young

EXERCISE 7.2

Words that are underlined are contracted.

Proverbs 23:17 Let <u>not</u> thine heart envy sinners: <u>but</u> be thou in <u>the</u> fear <u>of</u> <u>the</u> LORD all <u>the</u> <u>day</u> long.

Proverbs 12:19 <u>The</u> lip <u>of</u> truth shall be established <u>for</u> <u>ever</u>: but a lying tongue is <u>but</u> <u>for</u> a moment.

Mark 6:3 Is <u>not</u> this <u>the</u> carpenter, <u>the</u> son <u>of</u> Mary, <u>the</u> brother <u>of</u> James, <u>and</u> Joses, <u>and</u> <u>of</u> Juda, <u>and</u> Simon? <u>and</u> are <u>not</u> his sisters <u>here</u> <u>with</u> <u>us</u>? <u>And</u> they were offended at him.

Proverbs 4:1 <u>Hear</u>, ye children, <u>the</u> instruction <u>of</u> a <u>father</u>, <u>and</u> attend to <u>know</u> <u>under</u> standing.

Proverbs 18:10 <u>The</u> <u>name</u> <u>of</u> <u>the</u> LORD is a strong tower: <u>the</u> <u>right</u>eous runneth into <u>it</u>, <u>and</u> is safe.

Proverbs 15:12 A scorner loveth <u>not</u> <u>one</u> <u>that</u> reproveth him: neither <u>will</u> he <u>go</u> unto <u>the</u> wise.

1 Peter 4:14 If ye be reproached <u>for</u> <u>the</u> <u>name</u> <u>of</u> <u>Christ</u>, happy are ye; <u>for</u> <u>the</u> spirit <u>of</u> glory <u>and</u> <u>of</u> <u>God</u> resteth upon <u>you</u>: on their <u>part</u> he is evil spoken <u>of</u>, <u>but</u> on your <u>part</u> he is glorified.

1 Corinthians 10:27 If any <u>of</u> them <u>that</u> believe <u>not</u> bid <u>you</u> to a feast, <u>and</u> ye be disposed to <u>go</u>; what so <u>ever</u> is set before <u>you</u>, eat, asking no <u>question</u> <u>for</u> conscience sake.

Proverbs 4:16 <u>For</u> they sleep <u>not</u>, except they <u>have</u> <u>done</u> mischief; <u>and</u> their sleep is taken away, unless they cause <u>some</u> to fall.

Proverbs 25:19 Confidence in an unfaithful man in <u>time</u> <u>of</u> trouble is <u>like</u> a broken tooth, <u>and</u> a foot out <u>of</u> joint.

Proverbs 12:24 <u>The</u> hand <u>of</u> <u>the</u> diligent shall bear rule: <u>but</u> <u>the</u> slothful shall be <u>under</u> tribute.

Proverbs 20:11 Even a child is <u>known</u> by his doings, whether his <u>work</u> be pure, <u>and</u> whether <u>it</u> be <u>right</u>.

Proverbs 30:17 <u>The</u> eye <u>that</u> mocketh at his <u>father</u>, <u>and</u> despiseth to obey his <u>mother</u>, <u>the</u> ravens <u>of</u> <u>the</u> valley shall pick <u>it</u> out, <u>and</u> <u>the</u> <u>young</u> eagles shall eat <u>it</u>.

Exercise 8.1

Words that are underlined are contracted.

Psalm 127:4 As arrows are in <u>the</u> <u>hand</u> <u>of</u> a mighty man; so are children <u>of</u> <u>the</u> youth.

Psalm 86:5 <u>For</u> thou, Lord, art good, <u>and</u> ready to <u>forgive</u>; <u>and</u> plenteous in mercy unto all <u>them</u> that call upon <u>thee</u>.

Psalm 131:1 A Song <u>of</u> degrees <u>of</u> David. Lord, my heart is not haughty, nor mine eyes <u>lofty</u>: neither do I exercise myself in great matters, or in things too high <u>for</u> me.

Psalm 2:12 Kiss <u>the</u> Son, lest he be angry, <u>and</u> ye perish from <u>the</u> way, when his wrath is kindled but a little. Blessed are all <u>they</u> that put <u>their</u> trust in him.

Psalm 1:3 <u>And</u> he shall be like a tree planted by <u>the</u> rivers <u>of</u> water, that bringeth <u>forth</u> his fruit in his season; his leaf also shall not <u>wither</u>; <u>and</u> whatsoever he doeth shall prosper.

EXERCISE 8.2

2 Timothy 2:22 Flee also <u>youthful</u> lusts: <u>but</u> foll<u>ow</u> <u>righte</u>ousness, fai<u>th</u>, <u>c</u>harity, peace, <u>with</u> <u>them</u> <u>that</u> call on <u>the</u> <u>Lord</u> <u>out</u> <u>of</u> a pure heart.

Mark 1:22 <u>And</u> <u>they</u> <u>we</u>re astoni<u>shed</u> at his doctrine: <u>for</u> he taug<u>ht</u> <u>them</u> <u>as</u> <u>one</u> <u>that</u> had au<u>th</u>ority, <u>and</u> <u>not</u> <u>as</u> <u>the</u> scribes.

Luke 10:27 <u>And</u> he answe<u>ring</u> said, <u>Thou</u> <u>s</u>halt love <u>the</u> <u>Lord</u> <u>thy</u> <u>God</u> <u>with</u> all <u>thy</u> heart, <u>and</u> <u>with</u> all <u>thy</u> s<u>oul</u>, <u>and</u> <u>with</u> all <u>thy</u> streng<u>th</u>, <u>and</u> <u>with</u> all <u>thy</u> mind; <u>and</u> <u>thy</u> neigh<u>bour</u> <u>as</u> <u>thy</u>self.

Psalm 34:18 <u>The</u> <u>LORD</u> is nig<u>h</u> unto <u>them</u> <u>that</u> are <u>of</u> a broken heart; <u>and</u> save<u>th</u> such <u>as</u> be <u>of</u> a contrite spirit.

Ephesians 6:11 Put on <u>the</u> <u>w</u>hole arm<u>our</u> <u>of</u> <u>God</u>, <u>that</u> ye may be able to st<u>and</u> against <u>the</u> wiles <u>of</u> <u>the</u> devil.

Luke 14:8 <u>When</u> <u>thou</u> art bidden <u>of</u> any man to a we<u>dding</u>, sit <u>not</u> d<u>own</u> in <u>the</u> hig<u>h</u>est room; lest a <u>more</u> hon<u>our</u>able man <u>than</u> <u>thou</u> be bidden <u>of</u> him;

Mark 10:44 <u>And</u> <u>whoso</u>ever <u>of</u> <u>you</u> <u>will</u> be <u>the</u> <u>c</u>hiefest, <u>shall</u> be s<u>er</u>vant <u>of</u> all.

EXERCISE 9.1

2 Timothy 3:15 <u>And that from</u> a <u>child thou</u> hast <u>known</u> <u>the</u> holy scriptures, <u>which</u> are able to make <u>thee</u> wise unto salvation <u>through</u> fai<u>th</u> <u>which</u> is in <u>Christ</u> <u>Jesus</u>.

EXERCISE 9.2

Luke 5:21 <u>And</u> <u>the</u> scribes <u>and</u> <u>the</u> Pharisees began to reason, saying, <u>Who</u> is <u>this</u> <u>which</u> speak<u>eth</u> blasphemies? <u>Who</u> <u>can</u> <u>forgive</u> sins, <u>but</u> <u>God</u> al<u>one</u>?

EXERCISE 9.3

Psalm 8:2 <u>Out</u> <u>of</u> <u>the</u> <u>mouth</u> <u>of</u> babes <u>and</u> sucklings hast <u>thou</u> ordain<u>ed</u> streng<u>th</u> because <u>of</u> <u>thine</u> enemies, <u>that</u> <u>thou</u> migh<u>test</u> still <u>the</u> enemy <u>and</u> <u>the</u> aveng<u>er</u>.

EXERCISE 9.4

Matthew 4:4 <u>But</u> he answ<u>ered</u> <u>and</u> said, <u>It</u> is written, Man <u>shall</u> <u>not</u> live by bread al<u>one</u>, <u>but</u> by <u>every</u> word <u>that</u> proce<u>edeth</u> <u>out</u> <u>of</u> <u>the</u> <u>mouth</u> <u>of</u> God.

EXERCISE 10.1

<u>God</u>ly <u>character</u>, bas<u>ed</u> in tru<u>th</u> <u>and</u> <u>right</u>e<u>ous</u>ness, resulting in attitudes <u>of</u> fai<u>th</u>fulness, <u>thank</u>fulness, gratefulness, praise, contentment <u>and</u> <u>the</u> <u>like</u>. <u>Like</u> <u>the</u> learning tools <u>these</u> tools are develop<u>ed</u> in <u>us</u>. <u>Character</u> develops <u>through</u> <u>the</u> events <u>of</u> life - parents tea<u>ch</u> <u>the</u> biblical responses to <u>these</u> events. However, <u>it</u> is <u>not</u> tea<u>ch</u>ing <u>that</u> produces <u>character</u> <u>rather</u> <u>the</u> testings <u>of</u> life. <u>The</u> testings <u>of</u> life occur <u>through</u> interaction <u>with</u> parents, siblings, gr<u>and</u>parents, friends, etc.

(<u>S</u>ource: Mr Pet<u>er</u> Frogley's presentation on "Providing Tools <u>for</u> <u>our</u> Families" at <u>the</u> Adelaide CHESS Conf<u>er</u>ence 2009)

EXERCISE 11.1

Acts 20:35 I <u>have</u> shew<u>ed</u> <u>you</u> all <u>things</u>, <u>how</u> <u>that</u> <u>so</u> labouring ye <u>ought</u> to support <u>the</u> weak, <u>and</u> to rememb<u>er</u> <u>the</u> words <u>of</u> <u>the</u> Lord Jesus, <u>how</u> he said, <u>It</u> is <u>more</u> blessed to give <u>than</u> to receive.

1 Thessalonians 4:11 <u>And</u> <u>that</u> ye study to be quiet, <u>and</u> to <u>do</u> <u>your</u> <u>own</u> business, <u>and</u> to <u>work</u> <u>with</u> <u>your</u> <u>own</u> h<u>and</u>s, <u>as</u> we comm<u>and</u>ed <u>you</u>;

Titus 2:4 <u>That</u> <u>they</u> may tea<u>ch</u> <u>the</u> <u>young</u> women to be sob<u>er</u>, to love <u>their</u> husb<u>and</u>s, to love <u>their</u> <u>ch</u>ildren,

Titus 2:6 <u>Young</u> men likewise exhort to be sob<u>er</u> mind<u>ed</u>.

1 John 5:7 <u>For</u> <u>there</u> are <u>three</u> <u>that</u> bear record in heaven, <u>the</u> <u>Father</u>, <u>the</u> Word, <u>and</u> <u>the</u> Holy <u>Ghost</u>: <u>and</u> <u>these</u> <u>three</u> are <u>one</u>.

1 John 5:8 <u>And</u> <u>there</u> are <u>three</u> <u>that</u> bear witness in ear<u>th</u>, <u>the</u> Spirit, <u>and</u> <u>the</u> water, <u>and</u> <u>the</u> blood: <u>and</u> <u>these</u> <u>three</u> agree in <u>one</u>.

EXERCISE 12.1

1 Co Chapter 15, verses 51 to 52.

Behold, I shew you a mystery; We shall not all sleep, but we shall all be changed,

In a moment, in the twinkling of an eye, at the last trump: for the trumpet shall sound, and the dead shall be raised incorruptible, and we shall be changed.

For this corruptible must put on incorruption, and this mortal must put on immortality.

So when this corruptible shall have put on incorruption, and this mortal shall have put on immortality, then shall be brought to pass the saying that is written, Death is swallowed up in victory.

O death, where is thy sting? O grave, where is thy victory?

The sting of death is sin; and the strength of sin is the law.

But thanks be to God, which giveth us the victory through our Lord Jesus Christ.

EXERCISE 12.2

Revelation 4:11 Thou art worthy, O Lord, to receive glory and honour and power: for thou hast created all things, and for thy pleasure they are and were created.

John 11:27 She saith unto him, Yea, Lord: I believe that thou art the Christ, the Son of God, which should come into the world.

Psalm 46:10 Be still, and know that I am God: I will be exalted among the heathen, I will be exalted in the earth.

Mark 4:39 And he arose, and rebuked the wind, and said unto the sea, Peace, be still. And the wind ceased, and there was a great calm.

EXERCISE 12.3

John 6:66 to 69
From that time many of his disciples went back, and walked no more with him.
Then said Jesus unto the twelve, Will ye also go away?
Then Simon Peter answered him, Lord, to whom shall we go? thou hast the words of eternal life.
And we believe and are sure that thou art that Christ, the Son of the living God.

EXERCISE 13.1

Note: There are Braille contractions for "yourselves", "ourselves", "neither", "would", "should", "such", "their", "ount", "about", "thyself", "together" and "rejoiced" which we haven't learnt yet. So for now, we shall use the Braille signs for "ou" in yourselves, ourselves, would and should; and "th" and "er" in neither; "ch" in such; "the" in their and together; "ou" in count and about; "th" in thyself; and "ed" in rejoiced.

2 Thessalonians chapter 3, verses 6 to 15.

Now we command you, brethren, in the name of our Lord Jesus Christ, that ye withdraw yourselves from every brother that walketh disorderly, and not after the tradition which he received of us.

For yourselves know how ye ought to follow us: for we behaved not ourselves disorderly among you;

Neither did we eat any man's bread for nought; but wrought with labour and travail night and day, that we might not be chargeable to any of you:

Not because we have not power, but to make ourselves an ensample unto you to follow us.

For even when we were with you, this we commanded you, that if any would not work, neither should he eat.

For we hear that there are some which walk among you disorderly, working not at all, but are busybodies.

Now them that are such we command and exhort by our Lord Jesus Christ, that with quietness they work, and eat their own bread.

But ye, brethren, be not weary in well doing.

And if any man obey not our word by this epistle, note that man, and have no company with him, that he may be ashamed.

Yet count him not as an enemy, but admonish him as a brother.

EXERCISE 13.2

Proverbs 10:4 He becometh poor that dealeth with a slack hand: but the hand of the diligent maketh rich.

Proverbs 12:24 The hand of the diligent shall bear rule: but the slothful shall be under tribute.

Proverbs 12:27 The slothful man roasteth not that which he took in hunting: but the substance of a diligent man is precious.

Proverbs 13:4 The soul of the sluggard desireth, and hath nothing: but the soul of the diligent shall be made fat.

Proverbs 21:5 The thoughts of the diligent tend only to plenteousness; but of every one that is hasty only to want.

Proverbs 22:29 Seest thou a man diligent in his business? he shall stand before kings; he shall not stand before mean men.

1 Timothy 5:8 But if any provide not for his own, and specially for those of his own house, he hath denied the faith, and is worse than an infidel.

Proverbs 10:16 The labour of the righteous tendeth to life: the fruit of the wicked to sin.

Psalm 37:25 I have been young, and now am old; yet have I not seen the righteous forsaken, nor his seed begging bread.

EXERCISE 13.3

2 Timothy 2:14 to 16

Of these things put them in remembrance, charging them before the Lord that they strive not about words to no profit, but to the subverting of the hearers.

Study to shew thyself approved unto God, a workman that needeth not to be ashamed, rightly dividing the word of truth.

But shun profane and vain babblings: for they will increase unto more ungodliness.

Daniel chapter 3, verses 27 and 28

And the princes, governors, and captains, and the king's counsellors, being gathered together, saw these men, upon whose bodies the fire had no power, nor was an hair of their head singed, neither were their coats changed, nor the smell of fire had passed on them.

Then Nebuchadnezzar spake, and said, Blessed be the God of Shadrach, Meshach, and Abednego, who hath sent his angel, and delivered his servants that trusted in him, and have changed the king's word, and yielded their bodies, that they might not serve nor worship any god, except their own God.

EXERCISE 13.4

Luke chapter 1, verses 46 to 55

And Mary said, My soul doth magnify the Lord,

And my spirit hath rejoiced in God my Saviour.

For he hath regarded the low estate of his handmaiden: for, behold, from hence forth all generations shall call me blessed.

For he that is mighty hath done to me great things; and holy is his name.

And his mercy is on them that fear him from generation to generation.

He hath shewed strength with his arm; he hath scattered the proud in the imagination of their hearts.

He hath put down the mighty from their seats, and exalted them of low degree.

He hath filled the hungry with good things; and the rich he hath sent empty away.

He hath holpen his servant Israel, in remembrance of his mercy;

As he spake to our fathers, to Abraham, and to his seed for ever.

EXERCISE 14.1

1Ki 8:27 But will God indeed dwell on the earth? behold, the heaven and heaven of heavens cannot contain thee; how much less this house that I have builded?

Heb 11:5 By faith Enoch was translated that he should not see death; and was not found, because God had translated him: for before his translation he had this testimony, that he pleased God.

Matthew 26:26 to 30

And as they were eating, Jesus took bread, and blessed it, and brake it, and gave it to the disciples, and said, Take, eat; this is my body.

And he took the cup, and gave thanks, and gave it to them, saying, Drink ye all of it;

For this is my blood of the new testament, which is shed for many for the remission of sins.

But I say unto you, I will not drink henceforth of this fruit of the vine, until that day when I drink it new with you in my Father's kingdom.

And when they had sung an hymn, they went out into the mount of Olives.

EXERCISE 14.2

John 4:23 But the hour cometh, and now is, when the true worshippers shall worship the Father in spirit and in truth: for the Father seeketh such to worship him.

John 4:24 God is a Spirit: and they that worship him must worship him in spirit and in truth.

Mark chapter 8, verses 34 to 38

And when he had called the people unto him with his disciples also, he said unto them, Whosoever will come after me, let him deny himself, and take up his cross, and follow me.

For whosoever will save his life shall lose it; but whosoever shall lose his life for my sake and the gospel's, the same shall save it.

For what shall it profit a man, if he shall gain the whole world, and lose his own soul?

Or what shall a man give in exchange for his soul?

Whosoever therefore shall be ashamed of me and of my words in this adulterous and sinful generation; of him also shall the Son of man be ashamed, when he cometh in the glory of his Father with the holy angels.

EXERCISE 14.3

Eze 9:4 And the LORD said unto him, Go through the midst of the city, through the midst of Jerusalem, and set a mark upon the foreheads of the men that sigh and that cry for all the abominations that be done in the midst thereof.

Re 7:3 Saying, Hurt <u>not</u> <u>the</u> <u>ea</u>r<u>th</u>, nei<u>ther</u> <u>the</u> sea, nor <u>the</u> trees, till we <u>have</u> seal<u>ed</u> <u>the</u> <u>ser</u>vants <u>of</u> <u>our</u> <u>God</u> in <u>their</u> <u>fore</u>heads.

Re 9:4 <u>And</u> <u>it</u> was com<u>manded</u> <u>them</u> <u>that</u> <u>they</u> <u>should</u> <u>not</u> hurt <u>the</u> grass <u>of</u> <u>the</u> <u>ea</u>rth, nei<u>ther</u> any green <u>thing</u>, nei<u>ther</u> any tree; <u>but</u> only <u>those</u> men <u>which</u> <u>have</u> <u>not</u> <u>the</u> seal <u>of</u> <u>God</u> in <u>their</u> <u>fore</u>heads.

Re 13:16 <u>And</u> he caus<u>eth</u> all, bo<u>th</u> small <u>and</u> great, ri<u>ch</u> <u>and</u> poor, free <u>and</u> bond, to receive a mark in <u>their</u> <u>right</u> h<u>and</u>, or in <u>their</u> <u>fore</u>heads:

Re 14:1 <u>And</u> I look<u>ed</u>, <u>and</u>, lo, a Lamb <u>st</u>ood on <u>the</u> m<u>ou</u>nt Sion, <u>and</u> <u>with</u> him an hund<u>red</u> <u>for</u>ty <u>and</u> <u>four</u> <u>thousand</u>, hav<u>ing</u> his <u>Father</u>'s <u>name</u> written in <u>their</u> <u>fore</u>heads.

Re 20:4 <u>And</u> I saw <u>thr</u>one<u>s</u>, <u>and</u> <u>they</u> sat <u>upon</u> <u>them</u>, <u>and</u> judgment was given unto <u>them</u>: <u>and</u> I saw <u>the</u> s<u>ou</u>ls <u>of</u> <u>them</u> <u>that</u> <u>were</u> behead<u>ed</u> <u>for</u> <u>the</u> witness <u>of</u> <u>Jesus</u>, <u>and</u> <u>for</u> <u>the</u> <u>word</u> <u>of</u> <u>God</u>, <u>and</u> <u>which</u> <u>had</u> <u>not</u> wor<u>shipped</u> <u>the</u> bea<u>st</u>, nei<u>ther</u> his image, nei<u>ther</u> <u>had</u> receiv<u>ed</u> his mark <u>upon</u> <u>their</u> <u>fore</u>heads, or in <u>their</u> h<u>and</u>s; <u>and</u> <u>they</u> liv<u>ed</u> <u>and</u> reign<u>ed</u> <u>with</u> <u>Christ</u> a <u>thousand</u> year<u>s</u>.

Re 22:4 <u>And</u> <u>they</u> <u>shall</u> see his face; <u>and</u> his <u>name</u> <u>shall</u> be in <u>their</u> <u>fore</u>heads.

EXERCISE 15.1

Note: about, bound, must, such, ourselves, yourselves, your,

The "be", "con" and "dis" contractions can only be used at the beginning of words. The "be" contraction can also only be used when it forms its own syllable. Thus, in words such as been, best, bed, beast, bearing, etc, you can't use it.

Hebrews 13:1 to 17

Let bro<u>ther</u>ly love <u>con</u>tinue.

<u>Be</u> <u>not</u> <u>for</u>getful to en<u>ter</u>tain <u>strangers</u>: <u>for</u> <u>thereby</u> <u>some</u> <u>have</u> en<u>ter</u>tain<u>ed</u> angels unawares.

Remem<u>ber</u> <u>them</u> <u>that</u> <u>are</u> in bonds, <u>as</u> b<u>ound</u> <u>with</u> <u>them</u>; <u>and</u> <u>them</u> <u>which</u> suffer adver<u>s</u>ity, <u>as</u> <u>being</u> y<u>our</u>selves also in <u>the</u> body.

M<u>ar</u>riage is hon<u>ou</u>rable in all, <u>and</u> <u>the</u> b<u>ed</u> undefil<u>ed</u>: <u>but</u> <u>wh</u>oremongers <u>and</u> adul<u>ter</u>ers <u>God</u> <u>will</u> judge.

Let y<u>our</u> <u>con</u>versation <u>be</u> <u>with</u>out covet<u>ou</u>sness; <u>and</u> <u>be</u> <u>con</u>tent <u>with</u> <u>such</u> <u>things</u> <u>as</u> ye <u>have</u>: <u>for</u> he ha<u>th</u> said, I <u>will</u> ne<u>ver</u> leave <u>thee</u>, nor <u>for</u>sake <u>thee</u>.

<u>So</u> <u>that</u> we may boldly say, <u>The</u> <u>Lord</u> is my help<u>er</u>, <u>and</u> I <u>will</u> <u>not</u> fear <u>what</u> man <u>shall</u> <u>do</u> unto me.

Remember them which have the rule over you, who have spoken unto you the word of God: whose faith follow, considering the end of their conversation.

Jesus Christ the same yesterday, and today, and forever.

Be not carried about with divers and strange doctrines. For it is a good thing that the heart be established with grace; not with meats, which have not profited them that have been occupied therein.

We have an altar, whereof they have no right to eat which serve the tabernacle.

For the bodies of those beasts, whose blood is brought into the sanctuary by the high priest for sin, are burned without the camp.

Wherefore Jesus also, that he might sanctify the people with his own blood, suffered without the gate.

Let us go forth therefore unto him without the camp, bearing his reproach.

For here have we no continuing city, but we seek one to come.

By him therefore let us offer the sacrifice of praise to God continually, that is, the fruit of our lips giving thanks to his name.

But to do good and to communicate forget not: for with such sacrifices God is well pleased.
Obey them that have the rule over you, and submit yourselves: for they watch for your souls, as they that must give account, that they may do it with joy, and not with grief: for that is unprof -itable for you.

EXERCISE 15.2

2 Timothy 3:2 to 5

For men shall be lovers of their own selves, covetous, boasters, proud, blasphemers, disobedient to parents, unthankful, unholy,

Without natural affection, trucebreakers, false accusers, incontinent, fierce, despisers of those that are good,

Traitors, heady, highminded, lovers of pleasures more than lovers of God;
Having a form of godliness, but denying the power thereof: from such turn away.

Titus 3:3 For we ourselves also were sometimes foolish, disobedient, deceived, serving divers lusts and pleasures, living in malice and envy, hateful, and hating one another.

EXERCISE 16.1

Psalm 40:5 Many, O LORD my God, are thy wonderful works which thou hast done, and thy thoughts which are to us-ward: they cannot be reckoned up in order unto thee: if I would declare and speak of them, they are more than can be numbered.

Exodus 32:32 Yet now, if thou wilt forgive their sin—; and if not, blot me, I pray thee, out of thy book which thou hast written.

EXERCISE 17.1

Phillipians 2:1–11

If there be therefore any consolation in Christ, if any comfort of love, if any fellowship of the Spirit, if any bowels and mercies,

Fulfil ye my joy, that ye be likeminded, having the same love, being of one accord, of one mind.

Let nothing be done through strife or vainglory; but in lowliness of mind let each esteem other better than themselves.

Look not every man on his own things, but every man also on the things of others.

Let this mind be in you, which was also in Christ Jesus:

Who, being in the form of God, thought it not robbery to be equal with God:

But made himself of no reputation, and took upon him the form of a servant, and was made in the likeness of men:

And being found in fashion as a man, he humbled himself, and became obedient unto death, even the death of the cross.

Wherefore God also hath highly exalted him, and given him a name which is above every name:

That at the name of Jesus every knee should bow, of things in heaven, and things in earth, and things under the earth;

And that every tongue should confess that Jesus Christ is Lord, to the glory of God the Father.

Proverbs 6:6–11

Go to the ant, thou sluggard; consider her ways, and be wise:

Which having no guide, overseer, or ruler,

Provideth her meat in the summer, and gathereth her food in the harvest.

How long wilt thou sleep, O sluggard? when wilt thou arise out of thy sleep?

Yet a little sleep, a little slumber, a little folding of the hands to sleep:

So shall thy poverty come as one that travelleth, and thy want as an armed man.

Matthew 19:13–15

Then were there brought unto him little children, that he should put his hands on them, and pray: and the disciples rebuked them.

But Jesus said, Suffer little children, and forbid them not, to come unto me: for of such is the kingdom of heaven.

And he laid his hands on them, and departed thence.

EXERCISE 18.1

2 Corinthians 6:2 (For he saith, I have heard thee in a time accepted, and in the day of salvation have I succoured thee: behold, now is the accepted time; behold, now is the day of salvation.)

EXERCISE 19.1

Proverbs 3:19-20

The LORD by wisdom hath founded the earth; by understanding hath he established the heavens.

By his knowledge the depths are broken up, and the clouds drop down the dew.

Isaiah 40:18-25

To whom then will ye liken God? or what likeness will ye compare unto him?

The workman melteth a graven image, and the goldsmith spreadeth it over with gold, and casteth silver chains.

He that is so impoverished that he hath no oblation chooseth a tree that will not rot; he seeketh unto him a cunning workman to prepare a graven image, that shall not be moved.

Have ye not known? have ye not heard? hath it not been told you from the beginning? have ye not understood from the foundations of the earth?

It is he that sitteth upon the circle of the earth, and the inhabitants thereof are as grasshoppers; that stretcheth out the heavens as a curtain, and spreadeth them out as a tent to dwell in:

That bringeth the princes to nothing; he maketh the judges of the earth as vanity.

Yea, they shall not be planted; yea, they shall not be sown: yea, their stock shall not take root in the earth: and he shall also blow upon them, and they shall wither, and the whirlwind shall take them away as stubble.

To whom then will ye liken me, or shall I be equal? saith the Holy One.

EXERCISE 20.1

Proverbs 6:16-19

These six things doth the LORD hate: yea, seven are an abomination unto him:

A proud look, a lying tongue, and hands that shed innocent blood,

An heart that deviseth wicked imaginations, feet that be swift in running to mischief,

A false witness that speaketh lies, and he that soweth discord among brethren.

Exodus 9:26-35

Only in the land of Goshen, where the children of Israel were, was there no hail.

And Pharaoh sent, and called for Moses and Aaron, and said unto them, I have sinned this time: the LORD is righteous, and I and my people are wicked.

Intreat the LORD (for it is enough) that there be no more mighty thunderings and hail; and I will let you go, and ye shall stay no longer.

And Moses said unto him, As soon as I am gone out of the city, I will spread abroad my hands unto the LORD; and the thunder shall cease, neither shall there be any more hail; that thou mayest know how that the earth is the LORD's.

But as for thee and thy servants, I know that ye will not yet fear the LORD God.

And the flax and the barley was smitten: for the barley was in the ear, and the flax was bolled.

But the wheat and the rie were not smitten: for they were not grown up.

And Moses went out of the city from Pharaoh, and spread abroad his hands unto the LORD: and the thunders and hail ceased, and the rain was not poured upon the earth.

And when Pharaoh saw that the rain and the hail and the thunders were ceased, he sinned yet more, and hardened his heart, he and his servants.

And the heart of Pharaoh was hardened, neither would he let the children of Israel go; as the LORD had spoken by Moses.

Proverbs 30:15-17

The horseleach hath two daughters, crying, Give, give. There are three things that are never satisfied, yea, four things say not, It is enough:

The grave; and the barren womb; the earth that is not filled with water; and the fire that saith not, It is enough.

The eye that mocketh at his father, and despiseth to obey his mother, the ravens of the valley shall pick it out, and the young eagles shall eat it.

1 John 2:15-17

Love not the world, neither the things that are in the world. If any man love the world, the love of the Father is not in him.

For all that is in the world, the lust of the flesh, and the lust of the eyes, and the pride of life, is not of the Father, but is of the world.

And the world passeth away, and the lust thereof: but he that doeth the will of God abideth forever.

EXERCISE 21.1

Exodus 20:1-17

And God spake all these words, saying,

I am the LORD thy God, which have brought thee out of the land of Egypt, out of the house of bondage.

Thou shalt have no other gods before me.

Thou shalt not make unto thee any graven image, or any likeness of any thing that is in heaven above, or that is in the earth beneath, or that is in the water under the earth:

Thou shalt not bow down thyself to them, nor serve them: for I the LORD thy God am a jealous God, visiting the iniquity of the fathers upon the children unto the third and fourth generation of them that hate me;

And shewing mercy unto thousands of them that love me, and keep my commandments.

Thou shalt not take the name of the LORD thy God in vain; for the LORD will not hold him guiltless that taketh his name in vain.

Remember the sabbath day, to keep it holy.

Six days shalt thou labour, and do all thy work:

But the seventh day is the sabbath of the LORD thy God: in it thou shalt not do any work, thou, nor thy son, nor thy daughter, thy manservant, nor thy maidservant, nor thy cattle, nor thy stranger that is within thy gates:

For in six days the LORD made heaven and earth, the sea, and all that in them is, and rested the seventh day: wherefore the LORD blessed the sabbath day, and hallowed it.

Honour thy father and thy mother: that thy days may be long upon the land which the LORD thy God giveth thee.

Thou shalt not kill.

Thou shalt not commit adultery.

Thou shalt not steal.

Thou shalt not bear false witness against thy neighbour.

Thou shalt not covet thy neighbour's house, thou shalt not covet thy neighbour's wife, nor his manservant, nor his maidservant, nor his ox, nor his ass, nor any thing that is thy neighbour's.

EXERCISE 21.2

2 Peter 1:1-11

Simon Peter, a servant and an apostle of Jesus Christ, to them that have obtained like precious faith with us through the righteousness of God and our Saviour Jesus Christ:

Grace and peace be multiplied unto you through the knowledge of God, and of Jesus our Lord,

According as his divine power hath given unto us all things that pertain unto life and godliness, through the knowledge of him that hath called us to glory and virtue:

Whereby are given unto us exceeding great and precious promises: that by these ye might be partakers of the divine nature, having escaped the corruption that is in the world through lust.

And beside this, giving all diligence, add to your faith virtue; and to virtue knowledge;

And to knowledge temperance; and to temperance patience; and to patience godliness;

And to godliness brotherly kindness; and to brotherly kindness charity.

For if these things be in you, and abound, they make you that ye shall neither be barren nor unfruitful in the knowledge of our Lord Jesus Christ.

But he that lacketh these things is blind, and cannot see afar off, and hath forgotten that he was purged from his old sins.

Wherefore the rather, brethren, give diligence to make your calling and election sure: for if ye do these things, ye shall never fall:

For so an entrance shall be ministered unto you abundantly into the everlasting kingdom of our Lord and Saviour Jesus Christ.

EXERCISE 21.3

Galatians 5:13-6:10

For, brethren, ye have been called unto liberty; only use not liberty for an occasion to the flesh, but by love serve one another.

For all the law is fulfilled in one word, even in this; Thou shalt love thy neighbour as thyself.

But if ye bite and devour one another, take heed that ye be not consumed one of another.

This I say then, Walk in the Spirit, and ye shall not fulfil the lust of the flesh.

For the flesh lusteth against the Spirit, and the Spirit against the flesh: and these are contrary the one to the other: so that ye cannot do the things that ye would.

But if ye be led of the Spirit, ye are not under the law.

Now the works of the flesh are manifest, which are these; Adultery, fornication, uncleanness, lasciviousness,

Idolatry, witchcraft, hatred, variance, emulations, wrath, strife, seditions, heresies,

Envyings, murders, drunkenness, revellings, and such like: of the which I tell you before, as I have also told you in time past, that they which do such things shall not inherit the kingdom of God.

But the fruit of the Spirit is love, joy, peace, longsuffering, gentleness, goodness, faith,

Meekness, temperance: against such there is no law.

And they that are Christ's have crucified the flesh with the affections and lusts.

If we live in the Spirit, let us also walk in the Spirit.

Let us not be desirous of vain glory, provoking one another, envying one another.

Brethren, if a man be overtaken in a fault, ye which are spiritual, restore such an one in the spirit of meekness; considering thyself, lest thou also be tempted.

Bear ye one another's burdens, and so fulfil the law of Christ.

For if a man think himself to be something, when he is nothing, he deceiveth himself.

But let every man prove his own work, and then shall he have rejoicing in himself alone, and not in another.

For every man shall bear his own burden.

Let him that is taught in the word communicate unto him that teacheth in all good things.

Be not deceived; God is not mocked: for whatsoever a man soweth, that shall he also reap.

For he that soweth to his flesh shall of the flesh reap corruption; but he that soweth to the Spirit shall of the Spirit reap life everlasting.

And let us not be weary in well doing: for in due season we shall reap, if we faint not.

As we have therefore opportunity, let us do good unto all men, especially unto them who are of the household of faith.

EXERCISE 21.4

Revelation 13:11-18

And I beheld another beast coming up out of the earth; and he had two horns like a lamb, and he spake as a dragon.

And he exerciseth all the power of the first beast before him, and causeth the earth and them which dwell therein to worship the first beast, whose deadly wound was healed.

And he doeth great wonders, so that he maketh fire come down from heaven on the earth in the sight of men,

And deceiveth them that dwell on the earth by the means of those miracles which he had power to do in the sight of the beast; saying to them that dwell on the earth, that they should make an image to the beast, which had the wound by a sword, and did live.

And he had power to give life unto the image of the beast, that the image of the beast should both speak, and cause that as many as would not worship the image of the beast should be killed.

And he causeth all, both small and great, rich and poor, free and bond, to receive a mark in their right hand, or in their foreheads:

And that no man might buy or sell, save he that had the mark, or the name of the beast, or the number of his name.

Here is wisdom. Let him that hath understanding count the number of the beast: for it is the number of a man; and his number is Six hundred threescore and six.

EXERCISE 22.1 A

Ps 89:8 O LORD God of hosts, who is a strong LORD like unto thee? or to thy faithfulness round about thee?

Ps 8:1 To the chief Musician upon Gittith, A Psalm of David. O LORD our Lord, how excellent is thy name in all the earth! who hast set thy glory above the heavens.

Ps 150:2 Praise him for his mighty acts: praise him according to his excellent greatness.

Ps 104:21 <u>The</u> <u>young</u> lions ro<u>ar</u> <u>after</u> <u>their</u> prey, <u>and</u> seek <u>their</u> m<u>eat</u> <u>from</u> <u>God</u>.

Jud 19:8 <u>And</u> he <u>ar</u>ose <u>ear</u>ly <u>in</u> <u>the</u> mor<u>ning</u> on <u>the</u> fif<u>th</u> <u>day</u> to de<u>part</u>: <u>and</u> <u>the</u> damsel's <u>father</u> <u>said</u>, Com<u>fort</u> <u>thine</u> he<u>art</u>, I pray <u>thee</u>. <u>And</u> <u>they</u> <u>ta</u>rried until <u>afternoon</u>, <u>and</u> <u>they</u> did eat bo<u>th</u> <u>of</u> <u>them</u>.

Ps 73:24 <u>Thou</u> <u>s</u>halt guide me <u>with</u> <u>thy</u> c<u>ounsel</u>, <u>and</u> <u>afterward</u> <u>receive</u> me to glory.

Ps 37:21 <u>The</u> wick<u>ed</u> borr<u>ow</u>eth, <u>and</u> paye<u>th</u> <u>not</u> <u>again</u>: <u>but</u> <u>the</u> <u>righteous</u> <u>s</u>hewe<u>th</u> mercy, <u>and</u> give<u>th</u>.

Ps 34:16 <u>The</u> face <u>of</u> <u>the</u> <u>LORD</u> is <u>against</u> <u>them</u> <u>that</u> <u>do</u> evil, to cut <u>off</u> <u>the</u> remembr<u>ance</u> <u>of</u> <u>them</u> <u>from</u> <u>the</u> <u>earth</u>.

Ps 94:17 <u>Unless</u> <u>the</u> <u>LORD</u> <u>had</u> b<u>een</u> my help, my s<u>oul</u> <u>had</u> <u>almost</u> dwelt <u>in</u> sil<u>ence</u>.

John 3:18 He <u>that</u> <u>believeth</u> on <u>him</u> is <u>not</u> <u>condemned</u>: <u>but</u> he <u>that</u> <u>believeth</u> <u>not</u> is <u>condemned</u> <u>already</u>, <u>because</u> he ha<u>th</u> <u>not</u> <u>believed</u> <u>in</u> <u>the</u> <u>name</u> <u>of</u> <u>the</u> only <u>begotten</u> Son <u>of</u> <u>God</u>.

Ps 71:19 <u>Thy</u> <u>righteousness</u> <u>also</u>, O <u>God</u>, is <u>very</u> high, <u>who</u> has<u>t</u> <u>done</u> <u>great</u> things: O <u>God</u>, <u>who</u> is <u>like</u> unto <u>thee</u>!

Heb 4:3 <u>For</u> we <u>which</u> <u>have</u> <u>believed</u> <u>do</u> <u>enter</u> <u>into</u> rest, <u>as</u> he <u>said</u>, <u>As</u> I <u>have</u> sworn <u>in</u> my wra<u>th</u>, if <u>they</u> <u>s</u>hall <u>enter</u> <u>into</u> my re<u>st</u>: <u>although</u> <u>the</u> <u>w</u>orks <u>were</u> <u>finished</u> <u>from</u> <u>the</u> <u>foundation</u> <u>of</u> <u>the</u> <u>world</u>.

Ps 19:9 <u>The</u> fear <u>of</u> <u>the</u> <u>LORD</u> is cl<u>ean</u>, <u>enduring</u> <u>for</u> <u>ever</u>: <u>the</u> judgm<u>ents</u> <u>of</u> <u>the</u> <u>LORD</u> <u>are</u> true <u>and</u> <u>righteous</u> <u>altogether</u>.

Ps 103:9 He <u>will</u> <u>not</u> <u>always</u> <u>c</u>hide: <u>neither</u> <u>will</u> he keep <u>his</u> anger <u>for</u> <u>ever</u>.

Ps 37:7 Re<u>st</u> <u>in</u> <u>the</u> <u>LORD</u>, <u>and</u> wait pati<u>ently</u> <u>for</u> <u>him</u>: fret <u>not</u> <u>thyself</u> <u>because</u> <u>of</u> <u>him</u> <u>who</u> prosp<u>ereth</u> <u>in</u> <u>his</u> way, <u>because</u> <u>of</u> <u>the</u> man <u>who</u> br<u>i</u>nge<u>th</u> wick<u>ed</u> devices to pass.

Ps 98:6 <u>With</u> trumpets <u>and</u> s<u>ound</u> <u>of</u> cornet make a joy<u>ful</u> noise <u>before</u> <u>the</u> <u>LORD</u>, <u>the</u> King.

Ps 139:5 <u>Thou</u> has<u>t</u> b<u>eset</u> me <u>behind</u> <u>and</u> <u>before</u>, <u>and</u> laid <u>thine</u> hand <u>upon</u> me.

Jos 2:11 <u>And</u> <u>as</u> soon <u>as</u> we <u>had</u> heard <u>these</u> <u>things</u>, <u>our</u> hearts did melt, <u>neither</u> did <u>there</u> remain any <u>more</u> c<u>ourage</u> <u>in</u> any man, <u>because</u> <u>of</u> <u>you</u>: <u>for</u> <u>the</u> <u>LORD</u> <u>your</u> <u>God</u>, he is <u>God</u> <u>in</u> h<u>eaven</u> <u>above</u>, <u>and</u> <u>in</u> <u>earth</u> <u>beneath</u>.

Isa 43:11 I, ev<u>en</u> I, am <u>the</u> <u>LORD</u>; <u>and</u> <u>beside</u> me <u>there</u> is no sav<u>iour</u>.

Ps 99:1 <u>The</u> <u>LORD</u> reigne<u>th</u>; let <u>the</u> <u>people</u> tremble: he sitte<u>th</u> <u>between</u> <u>the</u> <u>c</u>herubims; let <u>the</u> <u>earth</u> <u>be</u> mov<u>ed</u>.

EXERCISE 22.1 B

Nu 24:13 If Balak <u>would</u> give me <u>his</u> h<u>ouse</u> full <u>of</u> silv<u>er</u> <u>and</u> gold, I <u>cannot</u> <u>go</u> <u>beyond</u> <u>the</u> com<u>m</u>a<u>ndment</u> <u>of</u> <u>the</u> <u>LORD</u>, to <u>do</u> <u>either</u> <u>good</u> or bad <u>of</u> m<u>ine</u> <u>own</u> mind; <u>but</u> what <u>the</u> <u>LORD</u> sai<u>th</u>, <u>that</u> <u>will</u> I spe<u>ak</u>?

Ps 78:5 <u>For</u> he <u>e</u>stabl<u>ished</u> a te<u>stimony</u> <u>in</u> Jacob, <u>and</u> appo<u>inted</u> a law <u>in</u> Israel, <u>which</u> he comm<u>anded</u> <u>our</u> <u>fathers</u>, <u>that</u> <u>they</u> <u>should</u> make <u>them</u> <u>known</u> to <u>their</u> <u>children</u>:

Ps 78:6 <u>That</u> <u>the</u> <u>generation</u> to come might <u>know</u> <u>them</u>, <u>even</u> <u>the</u> <u>children</u> <u>which</u> <u>should</u> <u>be</u> born; <u>who</u> <u>should</u> arise <u>and</u> <u>declare</u> <u>them</u> to <u>their</u> <u>children</u>:

Ps 51:5 Behold, I was shapen in iniquity; and in sin did my mother conceive me.

Isa 59:13 In transgressing and lying against the LORD, and departing away from our God, speaking oppression and revolt, conceiving and uttering from the heart words of falsehood.

Ro 16:18 For they that are such serve not our Lord Jesus Christ, but their own belly; and by good words and fair speeches deceive the hearts of the simple.

Jas 1:22 But be ye doers of the word, and not hearers only, deceiving your own selves.

Isa 46:10 Declaring the end from the beginning, and from ancient times the things that are not yet done, saying, My counsel shall stand, and I will do all my pleasure:

Pr 27:6 Faithful are the wounds of a friend; but the kisses of an enemy are deceitful.

Ps 34:8 O taste and see that the LORD is good: blessed is the man that trusteth in him.

Pr 31:22 She maketh herself coverings of tapestry; her clothing is silk and purple.

Ps 93:1 The LORD reigneth, he is clothed with majesty; the LORD is clothed with strength, wherewith he hath girded himself: the world also is stablished, that it cannot be moved.

Lev 25:5 That which groweth of its own accord of thy harvest thou shalt not reap, neither gather the grapes of thy vine undressed: for it is a year of rest unto the land.

Ge 1:11 And God said, Let the earth bring forth grass, the herb yielding seed, and the fruit tree yielding fruit after his kind, whose seed is in itself, upon the earth: and it was so.

Ro 7:6 But now we are delivered from the law, that being dead wherein we were held; that we should serve in newness of spirit, and not in the oldness of the letter.

Ps 2:12 Kiss the Son, lest he be angry, and ye perish from the way, when his wrath is kindled but a little. Blessed are all they that put their trust in him.

Mr 8:31 And he began to teach them, that the Son of man must suffer many things, and be rejected of the elders, and of the chief priests, and scribes, and be killed, and after three days rise again.

Isa 44:24 Thus saith the LORD, thy redeemer, and he that formed thee from the womb, I am the LORD that maketh all things; that stretcheth forth the heavens alone; that spreadeth abroad the earth by myself;

EXERCISE 22.1 C

Job 23:12 Neither have I gone back from the commandment of his lips; I have esteemed the words of his mouth more than my necessary food.

Ps 100:3 Know ye that the LORD he is God: it is he that hath made us, and not we ourselves; we are his people, and the sheep of his pasture.

Ezr 4:20 There have been mighty kings also over Jerusalem, which have ruled over all countries beyond the river; and toll, tribute, and custom, was paid unto them.

1 Jo 3:16 Hereby perceive we the love of God, because he laid down his life for us: and we ought to lay down our lives for the brethren.

Lu 9:47 And Jesus, perceiving the thought of their heart, took a child, and set him by him,

Ac 8:22 Repent therefore of this thy wickedness, and pray God, if perhaps the thought of thine heart may be forgiven thee.

Heb 12:28 Wherefore we receiving a kingdom which cannot be moved, let us have grace, whereby we may serve God acceptably with reverence and godly fear:

Ec 11:9 Rejoice, O young man, in thy youth; and let thy heart cheer thee in the days of thy youth, and walk in the ways of thine heart, and in the sight of thine eyes: but know thou, that for all these things God will bring thee into judgment.

Ps 19:8 The statutes of the LORD are right, rejoicing the heart: the commandment of the LORD is pure, enlightening the eyes.

Mt 6:19 Lay not up for yourselves treasures upon earth, where moth and rust doth corrupt, and where thieves break through and steal:

Mt 6:20 But lay up for yourselves treasures in heaven, where neither moth nor rust doth corrupt, and where thieves do not break through nor steal:

Exercise 22.2 A

Below are all the verses found in the Holy Bible to do with the blind.

Ex 4:11 And the LORD said unto him, Who hath made man's mouth? or who maketh the dumb, or deaf, or the seeing, or the blind? have not I the LORD?

Le 19:14 Thou shalt not curse the deaf, nor put a stumblingblock before the blind, but shalt fear thy God: I am the LORD.

Le 21:18 For whatsoever man he be that hath a blemish, he shall not approach: a blind man, or a lame, or he that hath a flat nose, or any thing superfluous,

Le 22:22 Blind, or broken, or maimed, or having a wen, or scurvy, or scabbed, ye shall not offer these unto the LORD, nor make an offering by fire of them upon the altar unto the LORD.

De 15:21 And if there be any blemish therein, as if it be lame, or blind, or have any ill blemish, thou shalt not sacrifice it unto the LORD thy God.

De 16:19 Thou shalt not wrest judgment; thou shalt not respect persons, neither take a gift: for a gift doth blind the eyes of the wise, and pervert the words of the righteous.

De 27:18 Cursed be he that maketh the blind to wander out of the way. And all the people shall say, Amen.

De 28:29 And thou shalt grope at noonday, as the blind gropeth in darkness, and thou shalt not prosper in thy ways: and thou shalt be only oppressed and spoiled evermore, and no man shall save thee.

1 Sa 12:3 Behold, here I am: witness against me before the LORD, and before his anointed: whose ox have I taken? or whose ass have I taken? or whom have I defrauded? whom have I oppressed? or of whose hand have I received any bribe to blind mine eyes therewith? and I will restore it you.

2 Sa 5:6 And the king and his men went to Jerusalem unto the Jebusites, the inhabitants of the land: which spake unto David, saying, Except thou take away the blind and the lame, thou shalt not come in hither: thinking, David cannot come in hither.

2 Sa 5:8 And David said on that day, Whosoever getteth up to the gutter, and smiteth the Jebusites, and the lame and the blind, that are hated of David's soul, he shall be chief and captain. Wherefore they said, The blind and the lame shall not come into the house.

EXERCISE 22.2 B

Job 29:15 I was eyes to the blind, and feet was I to the lame.

Ps 146:8 The LORD openeth the eyes of the blind: the LORD raiseth them that are bowed down: the LORD loveth the righteous:

Isa 29:18 And in that day shall the deaf hear the words of the book, and the eyes of the blind shall see out of obscurity, and out of darkness.

Isa 35:5 Then the eyes of the blind shall be opened, and the ears of the deaf shall be unstopped.

Isa 42:7 To open the blind eyes, to bring out the prisoners from the prison, and them that sit in darkness out of the prison house.

Isa 42:16 And I will bring the blind by a way that they knew not; I will lead them in paths that they have not known: I will make darkness light before them, and crooked things straight. These things will I do unto them, and not forsake them.

Isa 42:18 Hear, ye deaf; and look, ye blind, that ye may see.

Isa 42:19 Who is blind, but my servant? or deaf, as my messenger that I sent? who is blind as he that is perfect, and blind as the LORD's servant?

Isa 43:8 Bring forth the blind people that have eyes, and the deaf that have ears.

Isa 56:10 His watchmen are blind: they are all ignorant, they are all dumb dogs, they cannot bark; sleeping, lying down, loving to slumber.

Isa 59:10 We grope for the wall like the blind, and we grope as if we had no eyes: we stumble at noonday as in the night; we are in desolate places as dead men.

Jer 31:8 Behold, I will bring them from the north country, and gather them from the coasts of the earth, and with them the blind and the lame, the woman with child and her that travaileth with child together: a great company shall return thither.

La 4:14 They have wandered as blind men in the streets, they have polluted themselves with blood, so that men could not touch their garments.

Zep 1:17 And I will bring distress upon men, that they shall walk like blind men, because they have sinned against the LORD: and their blood shall be poured out as dust, and their flesh as the dung.

Mal 1:8 And if ye offer the blind for sacrifice, is it not evil? and if ye offer the lame and sick, is it not evil? offer it now unto thy governor; will he be pleased with thee, or accept thy person? saith the LORD of hosts.

EXERCISE 22.2 C

Mt 9:27 <u>And</u> <u>when</u> <u>J</u>esus de<u>parted</u> <u>thence</u>, two <u>blind</u> m<u>en</u> foll<u>owed</u> <u>him</u>, cry<u>ing</u>, <u>and</u> say<u>ing</u>, <u>Thou</u> Son <u>of</u> David, <u>have</u> m<u>e</u>rcy <u>on</u> <u>us</u>.

Mt 9:28 <u>And</u> <u>when</u> he <u>was</u> come <u>into</u> <u>the</u> h<u>ouse</u>, <u>the</u> <u>blind</u> m<u>en</u> came to <u>him</u>: <u>and</u> <u>J</u>esus sai<u>th</u> unto <u>th</u>em, Believe ye <u>that</u> I am able to <u>do</u> <u>this</u>? <u>They</u> <u>said</u> unto <u>him</u>, Yea, <u>Lord</u>.

Mt 11:5 <u>The</u> <u>blind</u> <u>receive</u> <u>their</u> sight, <u>and</u> <u>the</u> lame walk, <u>the</u> l<u>e</u>p<u>ers</u> <u>are</u> cl<u>ean</u>s<u>ed</u>, <u>and</u> <u>the</u> d<u>ea</u>f h<u>ear</u>, <u>the</u> d<u>ea</u>d <u>are</u> rais<u>ed</u> up, <u>and</u> <u>the</u> poor <u>have</u> <u>the</u> gospel pr<u>each</u>ed to <u>th</u>em.

Mt 12:22 <u>Then</u> <u>was</u> br<u>ought</u> unto <u>him</u> <u>one</u> possess<u>ed</u> <u>with</u> a devil, <u>blind</u>, <u>and</u> dumb: <u>and</u> he h<u>eal</u>ed <u>him</u>, in<u>so</u>mu<u>ch</u> <u>that</u> <u>the</u> <u>blind</u> <u>and</u> dumb bo<u>th</u> spake <u>and</u> saw.

Mt 15:14 Let <u>th</u>em al<u>one</u>: <u>they</u> <u>be</u> <u>blind</u> l<u>ea</u>d<u>ers</u> <u>of</u> <u>the</u> <u>blind</u>. <u>And</u> if <u>the</u> <u>blind</u> l<u>ea</u>d <u>the</u> <u>blind</u>, bo<u>th</u> <u>shall</u> fall <u>into</u> <u>the</u> dit<u>ch</u>.

Mt 15:30 <u>And</u> <u>great</u> multitudes came unto <u>him</u>, hav<u>ing</u> <u>with</u> <u>them</u> <u>those</u> <u>that</u> <u>were</u> lame, <u>blind</u>, dumb, maim<u>ed</u>, <u>and</u> <u>many</u> o<u>th</u>ers, <u>and</u> cas<u>t</u> <u>them</u> d<u>own</u> at <u>J</u>esus' feet; <u>and</u> he h<u>eal</u>ed <u>them</u>:

Mt 15:31 <u>In</u>so<u>much</u> <u>that</u> <u>the</u> multitude wond<u>ered</u>, <u>when</u> <u>they</u> saw <u>the</u> dumb to sp<u>eak</u>, <u>the</u> maim<u>ed</u> to <u>be</u> <u>whole</u>, <u>the</u> lame to walk, <u>and</u> <u>the</u> <u>blind</u> to see: <u>and</u> <u>they</u> glorif<u>ied</u> <u>the</u> <u>God</u> <u>of</u> Israel.

Mt 20:30 <u>And</u>, <u>be</u>hold, two <u>blind</u> men sitting by <u>the</u> way side, <u>when</u> <u>they</u> heard <u>that</u> <u>J</u>esus pass<u>ed</u> by, cri<u>ed</u> <u>out</u>, say<u>ing</u>, <u>Have</u> m<u>e</u>rcy <u>on</u> <u>us</u>, O <u>Lord</u>, <u>thou</u> Son <u>of</u> David.

Mt 21:14 <u>And</u> <u>the</u> <u>blind</u> <u>and</u> <u>the</u> lame came to <u>him</u> <u>in</u> <u>the</u> temple; <u>and</u> he h<u>eal</u>ed <u>them</u>.

Mt 23:16 Woe unto <u>you</u>, ye <u>blind</u> guides, <u>which</u> say, <u>Whoso</u><u>ever</u> <u>shall</u> sw<u>ear</u> by <u>the</u> temple, <u>it</u> is no<u>thing</u>; but <u>whoso</u><u>ever</u> <u>shall</u> sw<u>ear</u> by <u>the</u> gold <u>of</u> <u>the</u> temple, he is a debtor!

Mt 23:17 Ye fools <u>and</u> <u>blind</u>: <u>for</u> <u>whether</u> is <u>greater</u>, <u>the</u> gold, or <u>the</u> temple <u>that</u> sanctif<u>ieth</u> <u>the</u> gold?

Mt 23:19 Ye fools <u>and</u> <u>blind</u>: <u>for</u> <u>whether</u> is <u>greater</u>, <u>the</u> gift, or <u>the</u> alt<u>ar</u> <u>that</u> sanctif<u>ieth</u> <u>the</u> gift?

Mt 23:24 Ye <u>blind</u> guides, <u>which</u> <u>strain</u> at a gnat, <u>and</u> swall<u>ow</u> a camel.

Matthew 23:26 <u>Thou</u> <u>blind</u> Pharisee, cl<u>ea</u>nse <u>first</u> <u>that</u> <u>which</u> is <u>within</u> <u>the</u> cup <u>and</u> platt<u>er</u>, <u>that</u> <u>the</u> <u>out</u>side <u>of</u> <u>th</u>em may <u>be</u> cl<u>ea</u>n <u>also</u>.

Mr 8:22 <u>And</u> he come<u>th</u> to Be<u>th</u>saida; <u>and</u> <u>they</u> bring a <u>blind</u> man unto <u>him</u>, <u>and</u> b<u>es</u><u>ought</u> <u>him</u> to t<u>ou</u>ch <u>him</u>.

Mr 8:23 <u>And</u> he took <u>the</u> <u>blind</u> man by <u>the</u> hand, <u>and</u> led <u>him</u> <u>out</u> <u>of</u> <u>the</u> town; <u>and</u> <u>when</u> he <u>had</u> spit on <u>his</u> eyes, <u>and</u> put <u>his</u> hands <u>upon</u> <u>him</u>, he ask<u>ed</u> <u>him</u> if he saw <u>ought</u>.

Mr 10:46 <u>And</u> <u>they</u> came to <u>J</u>ericho: <u>and</u> <u>as</u> he we<u>nt</u> <u>out</u> <u>of</u> <u>J</u>eri<u>ch</u>o <u>with</u> <u>his</u> disciples <u>and</u> a <u>great</u> numb<u>er</u> <u>of</u> p<u>eople</u>, <u>blind</u> Bartimaeus <u>the</u> son <u>of</u> Timaeus, sat by <u>the</u> highway side begging.

Mr 10:49 <u>And</u> <u>J</u>esus stood <u>still</u>, <u>and</u> commanded <u>him</u> to <u>be</u> called. <u>And</u> <u>they</u> call <u>the</u> <u>blind</u> man, say<u>ing</u> unto <u>him</u>, <u>Be</u> <u>of</u> good comf<u>ort</u>, rise; he calle<u>th</u> <u>thee</u>.

Exercise 22.2 D

Mr 10:51 And Jesus answered and said unto him, What wilt thou that I should do unto thee? The blind man said unto him, Lord, that I might receive my sight.

Lu 4:18 The Spirit of the Lord is upon me, because he hath anointed me to preach the gospel to the poor; he hath sent me to heal the brokenhearted, to preach deliverance to the captives, and recovering of sight to the blind, to set at liberty them that are bruised,

Lu 6:39 And he spake a parable unto them, Can the blind lead the blind? shall they not both fall into the ditch?

Lu 7:21 And in that same hour he cured many of their infirmities and plagues, and of evil spirits; and unto many that were blind he gave sight.

Lu 7:22 Then Jesus answering said unto them, Go your way, and tell John what things ye have seen and heard; how that the blind see, the lame walk, the lepers are cleansed, the deaf hear, the dead are raised, to the poor the gospel is preached.

Lu 14:13 But when thou makest a feast, call the poor, the maimed, the lame, the blind:

Lu 14:21 So that servant came, and shewed his lord these things. Then the master of the house being angry said to his servant, Go out quickly into the streets and lanes of the city, and bring in hither the poor, and the maimed, and the halt, and the blind.

Luke 18:35 And it came to pass, that as he was come nigh unto Jericho, a certain blind man sat by the way side begging:

John 5:3 In these lay a great multitude of impotent folk, of blind, halt, withered, waiting for the moving of the water.

John 9:1 And as Jesus passed by, he saw a man which was blind from his birth.

John 9:2 And his disciples asked him, saying, Master, who did sin, this man, or his parents, that he was born blind?

John 9:6 When he had thus spoken, he spat on the ground, and made clay of the spittle, and he anointed the eyes of the blind man with the clay,

Exercise 22.2 E

John 9:8 The neighbours therefore, and they which before had seen him that he was blind, said, Is not this he that sat and begged?

John 9:13 They brought to the Pharisees him that aforetime was blind.

John 9:17 They say unto the blind man again, What sayest thou of him, that he hath opened thine eyes? He said, He is a prophet.

John 9:18 But the Jews did not believe concerning him, that he had been blind, and received his sight, until they called the parents of him that had received his sight.

John 9:19 <u>And</u> <u>they</u> ask<u>ed</u> <u>them</u>, say<u>ing</u>, Is <u>this</u> <u>your</u> son, <u>who</u> ye say <u>was</u> born <u>blind</u>? <u>how</u> <u>then</u> do<u>th</u> he <u>now</u> see?

John 9:20 <u>His</u> <u>parent</u>s answ<u>ered</u> <u>them</u> <u>and</u> <u>said</u>, We <u>know</u> <u>that</u> <u>this</u> is <u>our</u> son, <u>and</u> <u>that</u> he <u>was</u> born <u>blind</u>:

John 9:24 <u>Then</u> <u>again</u> call<u>ed</u> <u>they</u> <u>the</u> man <u>that</u> <u>was</u> <u>blind</u>, <u>and</u> <u>said</u> unto <u>him</u>, Give <u>God</u> <u>the</u> praise: we <u>know</u> <u>that</u> <u>this</u> man is a si<u>nner</u>.

John 9:25 He answ<u>ered</u> <u>and</u> <u>said</u>, <u>Whether</u> he <u>be</u> a si<u>nner</u> or no, I <u>know</u> <u>not</u>: <u>one</u> thing I <u>know</u>, <u>that</u>, <u>where</u>as I <u>was</u> <u>blind</u>, <u>now</u> I see.

John 9:32 <u>Since</u> <u>the</u> <u>world</u> <u>began</u> <u>was</u> <u>it</u> <u>not</u> <u>heard</u> <u>that</u> any man op<u>ened</u> <u>the</u> eyes <u>of</u> <u>one</u> <u>that</u> <u>was</u> born <u>blind</u>.

John 9:39 <u>And</u> <u>Jesus</u> said, <u>For</u> judg<u>ment</u> I am come <u>into</u> <u>this</u> <u>world</u>, <u>that</u> <u>they</u> <u>which</u> see <u>not</u> might see; <u>and</u> <u>that</u> <u>they</u> <u>which</u> see might <u>be</u> made <u>blind</u>.

John 9:40 <u>And</u> <u>some</u> <u>of</u> <u>the</u> Pharisees <u>which</u> <u>were</u> <u>with</u> <u>him</u> heard <u>these</u> <u>word</u>s, <u>and</u> <u>said</u> unto <u>him</u>, <u>Are</u> we <u>blind</u> <u>also</u>?

John 9:41 <u>Jesus</u> <u>said</u> unto <u>them</u>, If ye <u>were</u> <u>blind</u>, ye <u>should</u> <u>have</u> no sin: <u>but</u> <u>now</u> ye say, We see; <u>therefore</u> <u>your</u> sin remain<u>eth</u>.

John 10:21 O<u>ther</u>s <u>said</u>, <u>These</u> <u>are</u> <u>not</u> <u>the</u> <u>word</u>s <u>of</u> <u>him</u> <u>that</u> ha<u>th</u> a devil. <u>Can</u> a devil op<u>en</u> <u>the</u> eyes <u>of</u> <u>the</u> <u>blind</u>?

John 11:37 <u>And</u> <u>some</u> <u>of</u> <u>them</u> <u>said</u>, <u>Could</u> <u>not</u> <u>this</u> man, <u>which</u> op<u>ened</u> <u>the</u> eyes <u>of</u> <u>the</u> <u>blind</u>, have caus<u>ed</u> <u>that</u> even <u>this</u> man <u>should</u> <u>not</u> <u>have</u> died?

Ac 13:11 <u>And</u> <u>now</u>, <u>be</u>hold, <u>the</u> hand <u>of</u> <u>the</u> <u>Lord</u> is <u>upon</u> <u>thee</u>, <u>and</u> <u>thou</u> <u>shalt</u> <u>be</u> <u>blind</u>, <u>not</u> seeing <u>the</u> sun <u>for</u> a s<u>ea</u>son. <u>And</u> <u>immediately</u> <u>there</u> fell on <u>him</u> a mi<u>st</u> <u>and</u> a darkness; <u>and</u> he w<u>ent</u> <u>about</u> seek<u>ing</u> <u>some</u> to l<u>ead</u> <u>him</u> by <u>the</u> hand.

Ro 2:19 <u>And</u> <u>art</u> <u>confident</u> <u>that</u> <u>thou</u> <u>thyself</u> <u>art</u> a guide <u>of</u> <u>the</u> <u>blind</u>, a light <u>of</u> <u>them</u> <u>which</u> <u>are</u> <u>in</u> da<u>rkness</u>,

2 Pe 1:9 <u>But</u> he <u>that</u> lack<u>eth</u> <u>these</u> <u>things</u> is <u>blind</u>, <u>and</u> <u>cannot</u> see afa<u>r</u> <u>off</u>, <u>and</u> ha<u>th</u> <u>forgott</u><u>en</u> <u>that</u> he <u>was</u> purg<u>ed</u> <u>from</u> <u>his</u> old sin<u>s</u>.

Re 3:17 <u>Because</u> <u>thou</u> say<u>est</u>, I am ri<u>ch</u>, <u>and</u> <u>increas</u><u>ed</u> <u>with</u> goods, <u>and</u> <u>have</u> n<u>eed</u> <u>of</u> no<u>thing</u>; <u>and</u> <u>knowest</u> <u>not</u> <u>that</u> <u>thou</u> <u>art</u> wret<u>ched</u>, <u>and</u> mis<u>erable</u>, <u>and</u> poor, <u>and</u> <u>blind</u>, <u>and</u> nak<u>ed</u>:

EXERCISE 23.1

Isa 40:22 *<u>It</u> is* he <u>that</u> sitt<u>eth</u> <u>upon</u> <u>the</u> <u>circle</u> <u>of</u> <u>the</u> earth, <u>and</u> <u>the</u> <u>inhabit</u>ants <u>thereof</u> *<u>are</u>* as grasshop-pers; <u>that</u> stretch<u>eth</u> <u>out</u> <u>the</u> heav<u>en</u>s <u>as</u> a curt<u>ain</u>, <u>and</u> spread<u>eth</u> <u>them</u> <u>out</u> <u>as</u> a t<u>ent</u> to dwell <u>in</u>:

Isa 43:11 I, *<u>even</u>* I, *am* <u>the</u> <u>LORD</u>; <u>and</u> <u>beside</u> me *<u>there</u> is* no savi<u>our</u>.

Ps 100:3 <u>Know</u> ye <u>that</u> <u>the</u> <u>LORD</u> he *is* <u>God</u>: *<u>it</u> is* he *<u>that</u>* ha<u>th</u> made <u>us</u>, <u>and</u> <u>not</u> we <u>ourselves</u>; *we <u>are</u>* <u>his</u> people, <u>and</u> <u>the</u> sheep <u>of</u> <u>his</u> pa<u>st</u>ure.

EXERCISE 23.2 A

1 Timothy 2:1-3:16

1 I exhort therefore, that, first of all, supplications, prayers, intercessions, *and* giving of thanks, be made for all men;

2 For kings, and *for* all that are in authority; that we may lead a quiet and peaceable life in all godliness and honesty.

3 For this *is* good and acceptable in the sight of God our Saviour;

4 Who will have all men to be saved, and to come unto the knowledge of the truth.

5 For *there* is one God, and one mediator between God and men, the man Christ Jesus;

6 Who gave himself a ransom for all, to be testified in due time.

7 Whereunto I am ordained a preacher, and an apostle, (I speak the truth in Christ, *and* lie not;) a teacher of the Gentiles in faith and verity.

8 I will therefore that men pray every where, lifting up holy hands, without wrath and doubting.

9 In like manner also, that women adorn themselves in modest apparel, with shamefacedness and sobriety; not with broided hair, or gold, or pearls, or costly array;

10 But (which becometh women professing godliness) with good works.

11 Let the woman learn in silence with all subjection.

12 But I suffer not a woman to teach, nor to usurp authority over the man, but to be in silence.

13 For Adam was first formed, then Eve.

14 And Adam was not deceived, but the woman being deceived was in the transgression.

15 Notwithstanding she shall be saved in childbearing, if they continue in faith and charity and holiness with sobriety.

EXERCISE 23.2 B

1 This *is* a true saying, If a man desire the office of a bishop, he desireth a good work.

2 A bishop then must be blameless, the husband of one wife, vigilant, sober, of good behaviour, given to hospitality, apt to teach;

3 Not given to wine, no striker, not greedy of filthy lucre; but patient, not a brawler, not covetous;

4 One that ruleth well his own house, having his children in subjection with all gravity;

5 (For if a man know not how to rule his own house, how shall he take care of the church of God?)

6 Not a novice, lest being lifted up with pride he fall into the condemnation of the devil.

7 Moreover he must have a good report of them which are without; lest he fall into reproach and the snare of the devil.

8   Likewise *must* the deacons *be* grave, not doubletongued, not given to much wine, not greedy of filthy lucre;

9   Holding the mystery of the faith in a pure conscience.

10   And let these also first be proved; then let them use the office of a deacon, being *found* blameless.

11   Even so *must their* wives *be* grave, not slanderers, sober, faithful in all things.

12   Let the deacons be the husbands of one wife, ruling their children and their own houses well.

13   For they that have used the office of a deacon well purchase to themselves a good degree, and great boldness in the faith which is in Christ Jesus.

14   These things write I unto thee, hoping to come unto thee shortly:

15   But if I tarry long, that thou mayest know how thou oughtest to behave thyself in the house of God, which is the church of the living God, the pillar and ground of the truth.

16   And without controversy great is the mystery of godliness: God was manifest in the flesh, justified in the Spirit, seen of angels, preached unto the Gentiles, believed on in the world, received up into glory.

Endnotes

1. © The Fred Hollows Foundation Website: www.hollows.org.au.

2. Project Canterbury, Poems Hitherto Uncollected, New York: The Analectic Press, 1873.

3. Louis Benson (1855-1930) was a Presbyterian minister and a leading authority on hymnology. (See www.cyberhymnal.org/bio/b/e/n/benson_lf.htm. Accessed on March 29, 2011.)

4. American Foundation for the Blind.

5. *What Christianity Has Given the World* by Alvin J Schmidt, p. 49, ©2001, 2004 Alvin J. Schmidt.

6. Planned Parenthood is the leading organization promoting abortion in the U.S.

7. Margaret Sanger, Pivot of Civilization page 112 or online at www.gutenberg.org/files/1689/1689-h/1689-h.htm#2HCH0005.

8. www.feministsforchoice.com/the-sanger-keller-connection.htm, www.afb.org/Section.asp?SectionID=1&TopicID=193&SubTopicID=20&DocumentID=1097. Accessed on April 2, 2011.

9. Charles Darwin, *The Descent of Man* (1871 edition), vol. I, p. 168.

10. See my book *The Sufficiency of Scripture: The Key to Revival*, ©2010 Joseph Stephen. All Rights Reserved.

11. Genesis 1:27; Psalm 8:5-6.

12. Adapted from www.genforum.genealogy.com/spencer/messages/8319.html. Accessed January 22, 2011. www.aph.org/hall_fame/bios/nemeth_art1.html.

13. As the Twig Is Bent, www.nfb.org/Images/nfb/Publications/books/kernel1/AsTheTwigIsBent.html. Accessed on January 22, 2011.

14. Adapted from www.genforum.genealogy.com/spencer/messages/8319.html.

15. www.nacl.com.au/nacl/index.php?option=com_content&view=article&id=45:christian-heritage&catid=24:articles&Itemid=30.

16. www.braille.org/papers/lorimer/apndx1.html.